2002 Annual Report

*Migratory Bird
Conservation Commission*

The Migratory Bird Conservation Commission

Sections 2 of the Migratory Bird Conservation Act of February 18, 1929 (Act), as amended, established the Migratory Bird Conservation Commission.

Section 2. A Commission to be known as the Migratory Bird Conservation Commission, consisting of the Secretary of the Interior, as Chairman; the Administrator of the Environmental Protection Agency; the Secretary of Agriculture; two Members of the Senate, to be selected by the President of the Senate; and two Members of the House of Representatives, to be selected by the Speaker, is created and authorized to consider and pass upon any area of land, water, or land and water that may be recommended by the Secretary of the Interior for purchase or rental under this Act and to fix the price or prices at which such area may be purchased or rented; and no purchase or rental shall be made of any such area until it has been duly approved for purchase or rental by said Commission. Any Member of the House of Representatives who is a member of the Commission, if reelected to the succeeding Congress, may serve on the Commission notwithstanding the expiration of a Congress. Any vacancy on the Commission shall be filled in the same manner as the original appointment. The ranking officer of the branch or department of a State to which is committed the administration of its game laws, or his authorized representative, shall be a member ex officio of said Commission for the purpose of considering and voting on all questions relating to the acquisition, under said sections, of areas in his State. For purposes of said sections, the purchase or rental of any area of land, water, or land and water includes the purchase or rental of any interest in any such area of land, water, or land and water.

Membership

Hon. Gale Norton
Secretary of the Interior, Chairman

Hon. Ann M. Veneman
Secretary of Agriculture

Hon. Christine Todd-Whitman
Administrator, Environmental Protection Agency

Hon. John B. Breaux
Senator from Louisiana

Hon. Thad Cochran
Senator from Mississippi

Hon. John D. Dingell
Representative from Michigan

Hon. Curt Weldon
Representative from Pennsylvania

Jeffery M. Donahoe
Secretary to the Commission
(October, 2001 through June, 2002)

A. Eric Alvarez
Acting Secretary to the Commission
(July through September 2002)

Telephone: 703/358 1716

Report of the Migratory Bird Conservation Commission for the Fiscal Year 2002

Front Cover: 2001-2002 Duck Stamp Artwork—Pintail
(Painting by Robert Hautman)

Approvals During Fiscal Year 2002

In Fiscal Year 2002, the Migratory Bird Conservation Commission approved the acquisition boundary at one national wildlife refuge. This refuge, totaling 16,437 acres, is the Red River National Wildlife Refuge in Caddo, Desoto, Red River and Natchitoches Parishes, Louisiana. It is authorized by Public Law 106- 300 and was established on August 22, 2002, with the acquisition of 3,857 acres. The Commission approved boundary additions, totaling 5,629 acres, to two refuges that were previously approved by the Commission. The Commission also approved the purchase price of 16,228 acres at 16 refuges and reapproved the price for fee lands at one refuge and leases at two refuges totaling 93,459 acres.

Area Approvals—New Areas

State	Area	New Area Acres
Louisiana	Red River NWR	16,437
Total		**16,437**

Area Approvals—Additions

State	Area	Addition Acres
Maryland	Blackwater NWR	500
Texas	Trinity River NWR	5,129
Total		**5,629**

Price Approvals

State	Area	Price Approval Acres
Arkansas	Bald Knob NWR	50
Arkansas	Cache River NWR	4,362
California	Lower Klamath NWR	329
California	North Central Valley WMA	119
Georgia	Savannah NWR	126
Louisiana	Red River	1,377
Maryland	Blackwater NWR	500
Mississippi	Tallahatchie NWR	120
New Jersey/New York	Wallkill River NWR	78
North Carolina/Virginia	Mackay Island NWR	20
North Carolina	Roanoke River NWR	3,063
Tennessee	Lower Hatchie NWR	161
Texas	Trinity River NWR	5,179
Virginia	Back Bay NWR	93
Washington	Conboy Lake NWR	331
Wyoming	Cokeville Meadows NWR (lease)	320
Total		**16,228**

Price Reapprovals

State	Area	Price Approval Acres
Arkansas	Cache River NWR	92,179
Louisiana	Lacassine NWR (lease)	640
Mississippi	Panther Swamp NWR (lease)	640
Total		**93,459**

The Migratory Bird Conservation Fund

The Migratory Bird Conservation Fund provides the Department of the Interior with monies to acquire migratory bird habitat. There are four major sources of money for the Fund. The most well-known source is the revenue received from the sale of Migratory Bird Hunting and Conservation Stamps, commonly known as Duck Stamps, as provided for under the Migratory Bird Hunting and Conservation Stamp Act of March 18, 1934, as amended. The other three major sources include appropriations authorized by the Wetlands Loan Act of October 4, 1961, as amended; import duties collected on arms and ammunition; and receipts from the sale of refuge admission permits as provided for in the Emergency Wetlands Resources Act of 1986. The Fund is further supplemented by receipts from the sale of products from refuge lands and rights-of-ways across national wildlife refuges, the disposal of refuge lands, and reverted Federal Aid funds.

Two land acquisition programs are financed from the Migratory Bird Conservation Fund. The first purchases major areas for migratory birds under the authority of the Migratory Bird Conservation Act. Lands acquired through this program are considered and approved by the Migratory Bird Conservation Commission. The second program acquires small natural wetlands and associated uplands located mainly in the Prairie Pothole Region of the upper Midwest. These lands, known as Waterfowl Production Areas, are acquired under the authority of the Migratory Bird Hunting and Conservation Stamp Act and do not require approval from the Commission.

During Fiscal Year 2002, the Department of the Interior obligated a total of $19,514,319 for the acquisition of land and interests in land totaling 34,129 acres in major migratory bird conservation areas. An additional $15,617,007 was obligated for projects in Waterfowl Production Areas totaling 58,156 acres.

A total of $46,930,082 was available for obligation from the Migratory Bird Conservation Fund during Fiscal Year 2002. Obligations for all Migratory Bird Conservation Fund land acquisition functions during the fiscal year totaled $46,531,702 ($715,842 of which were from prior year recoveries). The total obligations equal 99 percent of the available funds.

Summary of FY 2002
MBCF Land Acquisitions
Land Contracted for Purchase or Lease

National Wildlife Refuges: Purchase

State	Area	Acres
Arkansas	Bald Knob	50
Arkansas	Cache River	1,677
Arkansas	Overflow	80
California	Grasslands WMA (easements)	580
California	Humbolt Bay	30
California/Oregon	Lower Klamath	329
California	North Central Valley WMA	119
California	North Central Valley WMA (easements)	181
Georgia	Savannah	145
Louisiana	Red River	1,377
Louisiana	Upper Ouachita	1,174
New York	Montezuma	50
Maine	Moosehorn	2,036
Maryland	Blackwater	2,229
Massachusetts	Great Meadows	2
Mississippi	Coldwater River	307
New Jersey	Cape May	119
New Jersey	Edwin B. Forsythe	224
New York/New Jersey	Wallkill River	75
Oklahoma	Little River	460
Tennessee	Lower Hatchie	161
Texas	Laguna Atascosa	6,407
Texas	Trinity River	4,276
Washington	Conboy Lake	331
Total		**22,419**

National Wildlife Refuges: Lease

State	Area	Acres
Colorado	Browns Park	636
Louisiana	Lacassine	640
Louisiana	Upper Ouachita	3,217
Mississippi	Dahomey	260
Mississippi	Panther Swamp	640
Mississippi	St. Catherine Creek	502
Montana	Half Breed Lake	640
Montana	Lost Trail	1,022
Utah	Ouray	3,833
Wyoming	Cokeville Meadows	320
Total		**11,710**

Waterfowl Production Areas

State	Types of Acquisition	Acres
Iowa	Fee	1,055
Minnesota	Fee	2,379
Minnesota	Easement	4,696
Montana	Fee	881
Montana	Easement	5,172
Nebraska	Fee	163
North Dakota	Fee	639
North Dakota	Easement	6,314
South Dakota	Fee	1,637
South Dakota	Easement	34,867
Wisconsin	Fee	353
Total		**58,156**
Grand Total		**92,285**

New National Wildlife Refuge Boundary Approvals

In Fiscal Year 2002, the Migratory Bird Conservation Commission approved the acquisition boundary of one new refuge, the Red River National Wildlife Refuge in Caddo, Bossier, Desoto, Red River and Natchitoches Parishes, Louisiana. The Commission also approved the acquisition boundary of two national wildlife refuges that were previously established: the Blackwater National Wildlife Refuge in Dorchester County, Maryland; and the Trinity River National Wildlife Refuge in Liberty County, Texas.

Red River National Wildlife Refuge
Caddo, Bossier, Desoto, Red River, and Natchitoches Parishes, Louisiana

The Red River National Wildlife Refuge was authorized by Public Law 106-300 on October 13, 2000, and was established on August 22, 2002, under the Migratory Bird Conservation Act. The Secretary is authorized to acquire up to 50,000 acres in the project area which is located in northwest Louisiana along a 280-mile stretch of the Red River.

The Red River NWR will provide wintering habitat for mallards, pintails and wood ducks and contribute to the goals of the North American Waterfowl Management Plan. The bottomland hardwood forests of the Red River Valley have been almost totally cleared. Reforestation and restoration of native habitat will benefit a wide array of species. The Red River Valley is part of a major continental migration corridor for migratory birds funneling through the mid continent. The Red River NWR offers recreational, research and education opportunities for students, scientists, bird watchers, hunters and anglers.

The Commission approved the 16,437-acre boundary on June 12, 2002.

Red River National Wildlife Refuge
Cadda Bossier, Desota, Red River, and Natchitoches Parishes, Louisiana

SPANISH LAKE LOWLANDS UNIT

UNITED STATES
DEPARTMENT OF THE INTERIOR

UNITED STATES
FISH AND WILDLIFE SERVICE

LEGEND

BOUNDARY TO BE APPROVED

FOR APPROVAL-FEE

DATE OF MBCC MEETING

JAN 1 2 2002

SPECIAL PURPOSE MBCC

MEAN
DECLINATION

NAD 27
ZONE 15
UTM

COMPILED IN THE DIVISION OF REALTY
FROM SURVEYS BY U. S. G. S.

ATLANTA, GEORGIA   APRIL, 2002

0   3000   6000   9000   12000 FEET
0   1000 2000   3000 METERS

T 10 N
T 9 N

R 9 W   R 8 W   R 7 W

7

Blackwater National Wildlife Refuge
Dorchester County, Maryland

The Blackwater National Wildlife Refuge was established in 1932 as a waterfowl sanctuary. Lands were subsequently added through purchases and donations. The area around the Blackwater National Wildlife Refuge is undergoing major land use changes. Timber harvesting and land clearing for agricultural use are reducing the available habitat and degrading preservation of the refuge. The boundary expansion will aid in the preservation of the refuge and protect the highly productive and ecologically diverse wetlands from major environmental alternation and degradation associated with the saltwater intrusion.

The refuge is located approximately 14 miles south of Cambridge, Maryland, in south central Dorchester County. The addition includes approximately 500 acres located just south of Taylors Island Road and has over 500 feet of frontage on Parsons Creek. The area consists mostly of forested wetlands, interspersed with tidal waters, ponds and marsh. It provides nesting habitat for various waterfowl species, including black duck, mallard, blue-winged teal, gadwall and Canada geese. It also provides migration and wintering habitat for other waterfowl, such as pintail, green-winged teal, shovelers, mergansers, and tundra swans. Numerous species of other migratory birds, including the federally threatened bald eagle, songbirds, and webless waterbirds also utilize this area for nesting, roosting and foraging.

The Commission approved the 500 acre refuge boundary on March 14, 2002.

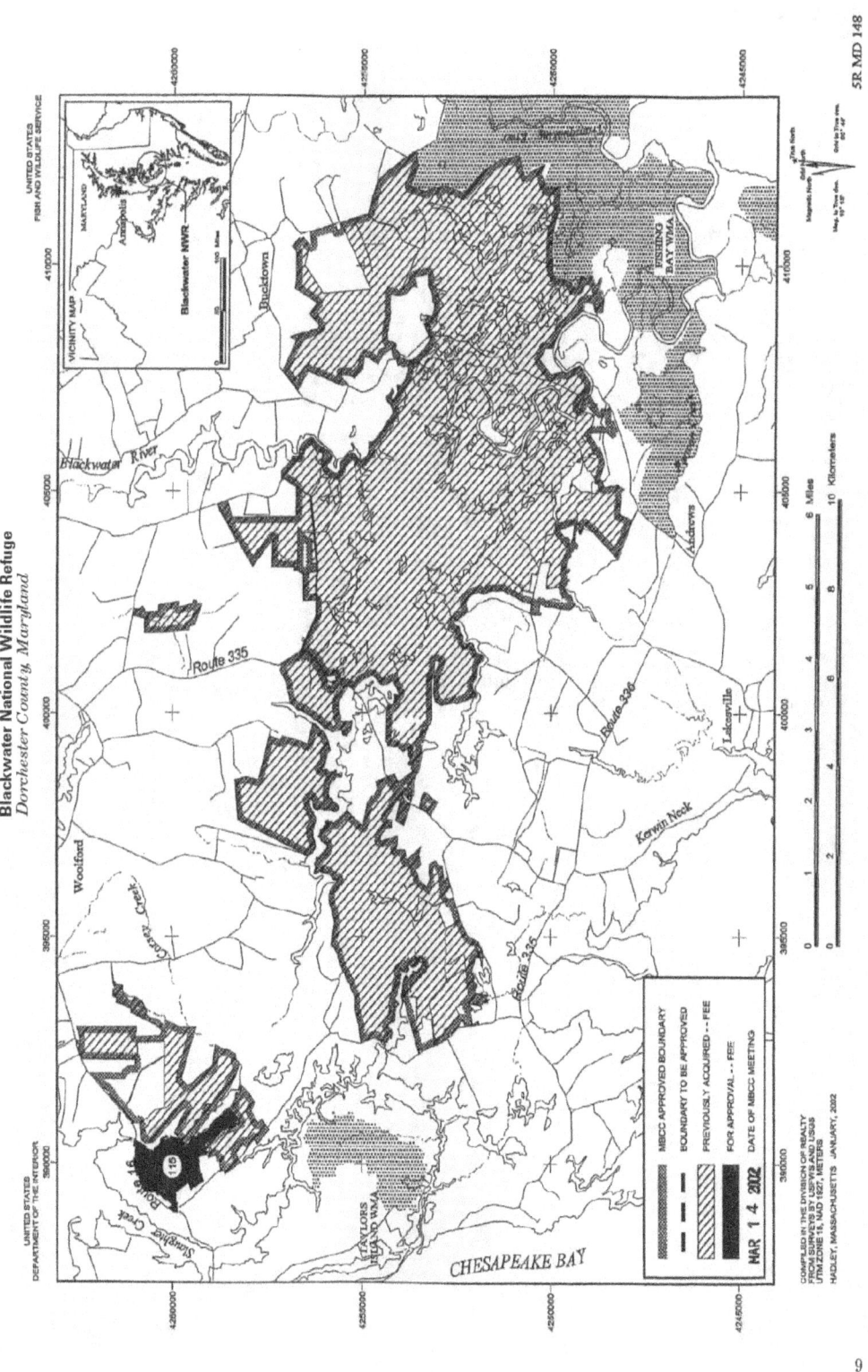

Blackwater National Wildlife Refuge
Dorchester County, Maryland

UNITED STATES
DEPARTMENT OF THE INTERIOR

UNITED STATES
FISH AND WILDLIFE SERVICE

CHESAPEAKE BAY

MBCC APPROVED BOUNDARY
BOUNDARY TO BE APPROVED
PREVIOUSLY ACQUIRED - - FEE
FOR APPROVAL - - FEE
DATE OF MBCC MEETING

MAR 1 4 2002

COMPILED BY THE DIVISION OF REALTY
FROM SURVEYS BY LEWIS AND ASSOC
UTM ZONE 18, NAD 1927, METERS

HADLEY, MASSACHUSETTS JANUARY, 2002

SR MD 148

VICINITY MAP

MARYLAND

Assateague

Blackwater NWR

9

Trinity River National Wildlife Refuge
Liberty County, Texas

The Trinity River National Wildlife Refuge was established on January 3, 1994, with the purchase of 4,400 acres of bottomland hardwood and associated habitats using Land and Water Conservation Fund appropriations. On June 14, 1994, the Migratory Bird Conservation Commission approved the initial MBCC boundary for the refuge, encompassing 20,110 acres. Since 1994, the MBCC boundary was expanded to include another 4,325 acres.

The refuge is located in Liberty County, Texas, about 45 miles northeast of Houston. It was created to protect remnant bottomland hardwood forests and associated wetland habitats for migrating, wintering, and breeding waterfowl. It currently represents one of the few remaining high-quality areas for waterfowl in east Texas. The high variety of wetlands on the project area provide important foraging and/or roosting habitat for the wood duck, mallard, gadwall, widgeon, green and blue-winged teal, lesser scaup and mottled ducks. The mature cavity trees dispersed throughout the area also provide important nesting habitat for wood ducks and black-bellied whistling ducks. Large colonial waterbird rookeries are abundant in the many swamps, sloughs and oxbow lakes found here. The expanded boundary allows for the acquisition of tracts in the Tanner Bayou and Capers Ridge Focus Areas of the Lower Trinity River Floodplain Stewardship Program as well as the Texas Bottomland Hardwood Initiative, a component of the Lower Mississippi Valley Joint Venture.

The Commission approved the 5,129-acre addition to the refuge boundary on June 12, 2002.

Trinity River National Wildlife Refuge
Liberty County, Texas

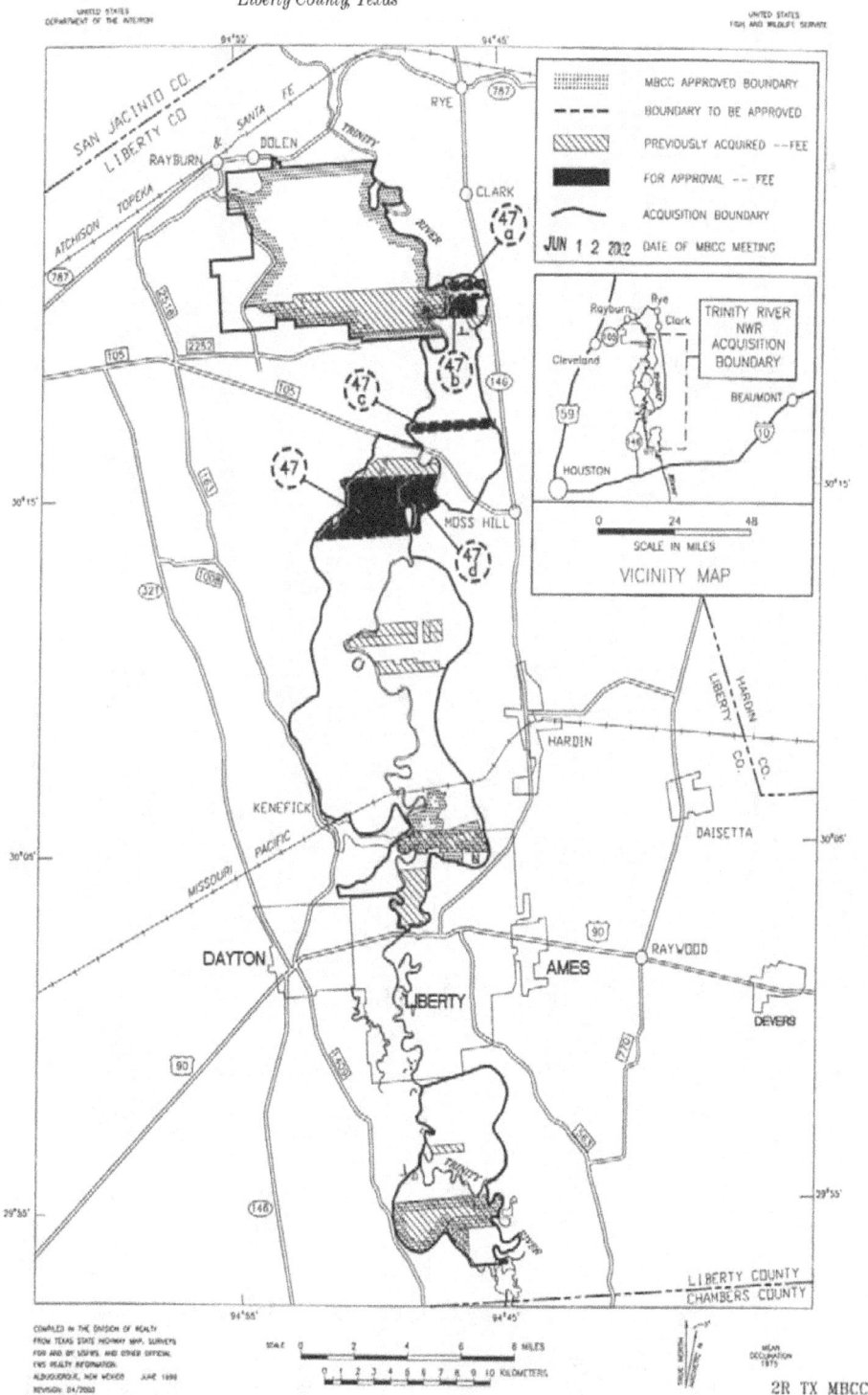

Membership of the National Migratory Bird Conservation Commission

Fiscal Year	Secretary of the Interior[1]	Secretary of Agriculture[2]	Secretary of Commerce[3]	Secretary of Transportation[4]	Administrator of Environmental Protection Agency[5]	Members on Part of the Senate		Members on Part of the House		Secretary to the Commission
1929	Ray L. Wilbur	Arthur M. Hyde	Robert P. Lamont			Peter Norbeck	Harry B. Hawes	Sam D. McReynolds	Ernest R. Ackerman	Rudolph Dieffenbach
1930										
1931									August H. Andresen	
1932		Henry A. Wallace	Roy D. Chapin						Roy O. Woodruff	
1933	Harold L. Ickes		Daniel C. Roper				Key Pittman		Chester C. Bolton	
1934										
1935										
1936									James Wolfenden	
1937						Charles L. McNary				
1938										
1939			Harry L. Hopkins				George L. Radcliffe	John J. Cochran		
1940		Claude R. Wickard	Jesse H. Jones							
1941									Walter E. Brehm	
1942										
1943										
1944						Vacant				Arthur A. Riemer
1945	Julius A. Krug	Clinton P. Anderson	Henry A. Wallace			C. Wayland Brooks	A. Willis Robertson			
1946										
1947			W. Averell Harriman					Frank M. Karsten		
1948		Charles F. Brannan	Charles W. Sawyer			Vacant / Raymond E. Baldwin				
1949						John W. Bricker				
1950	Oscar L. Chapman								August H. Andresen	
1951										
1952										
1953	Douglas McKay	Ezra Taft Benson	Sinclair Weeks							
1954										
1955							Thomas C. Hennings, Jr.			
1956	Fred A. Seaton									
1957									Leon H. Gavin	Albert J. Riesman
1958			Lewis L. Strauss			Roman L. Hruska	Lee Metcalf			
1959			Frederick H. Mueller							
1960										
1961	Stewart L. Udall	Orville L. Freeman	Luther H. Hodges							
1962										
1963									George A. Goodling	
1964									Silvio O. Conte	F. G. Spoden, Jr.
1965			John T. Connor					John D. Dingell		
1966										
1967			Alexander B. Trowbridge	Alan S. Boyd						
1968										
1969	Walter J. Hickel	Clifford M. Hardin		John A. Volpe		Henry L. Bellmon	Joseph D. Tydings			Walter R. McAllester
1970										
1971	Rogers C. B. Morton	Earl L. Butz					Lee Metcalf			
1972										
1973				Claude S. Brinegar						
1974										
1975	Stanley K. Hathaway			William T. Coleman			Quentin N. Burdick			
1976	Thomas S. Kleppe									
1977	Cecil D. Andrus	Bob Bergland		Brock Adams			Floyd K. Haskell			
1978										
1979				Neil Goldschmidt		Thad Cochran	David H. Pryor			
1980				Drew Lewis						
1981	James G. Watt	James R. Block							Richard T. Schulze	William F. Hartwig
1982										
1983	William P. Clark			Elizabeth H. Dole						
1984	Donald P. Hodel									
1985										
1986		Richard Lyng								
1987				James Burnley IV						
1988				Samuel K. Skinner						
1989	Manuel Lujan Jr.	Clayton Yeutter			William K. Reilly					
1990							John B. Breaux			
1991		Edward R. Madigan							Curt Weldon	Geoffrey L. Haskett
1992										
1993	Bruce Babbitt	Mike Espy			Carol M. Browner					
1994										
1995		Daniel R. Glickman								
1996										
1997										
1998										
1999										
2000										
2001	Gale Norton	Ann M. Veneman			Christine Todd-Whitman					Jeffery M. Donahue
2002										

1 Chairman 1940 to date
2 Chairman 1929 to 1939
3 Member 1929 to March 1, 1968
4 Member March 2, 1968 to December 12, 1989
5 Member December 13, 1989 to date

Trinity River National Wildlife Refuge
Liberty County, Texas

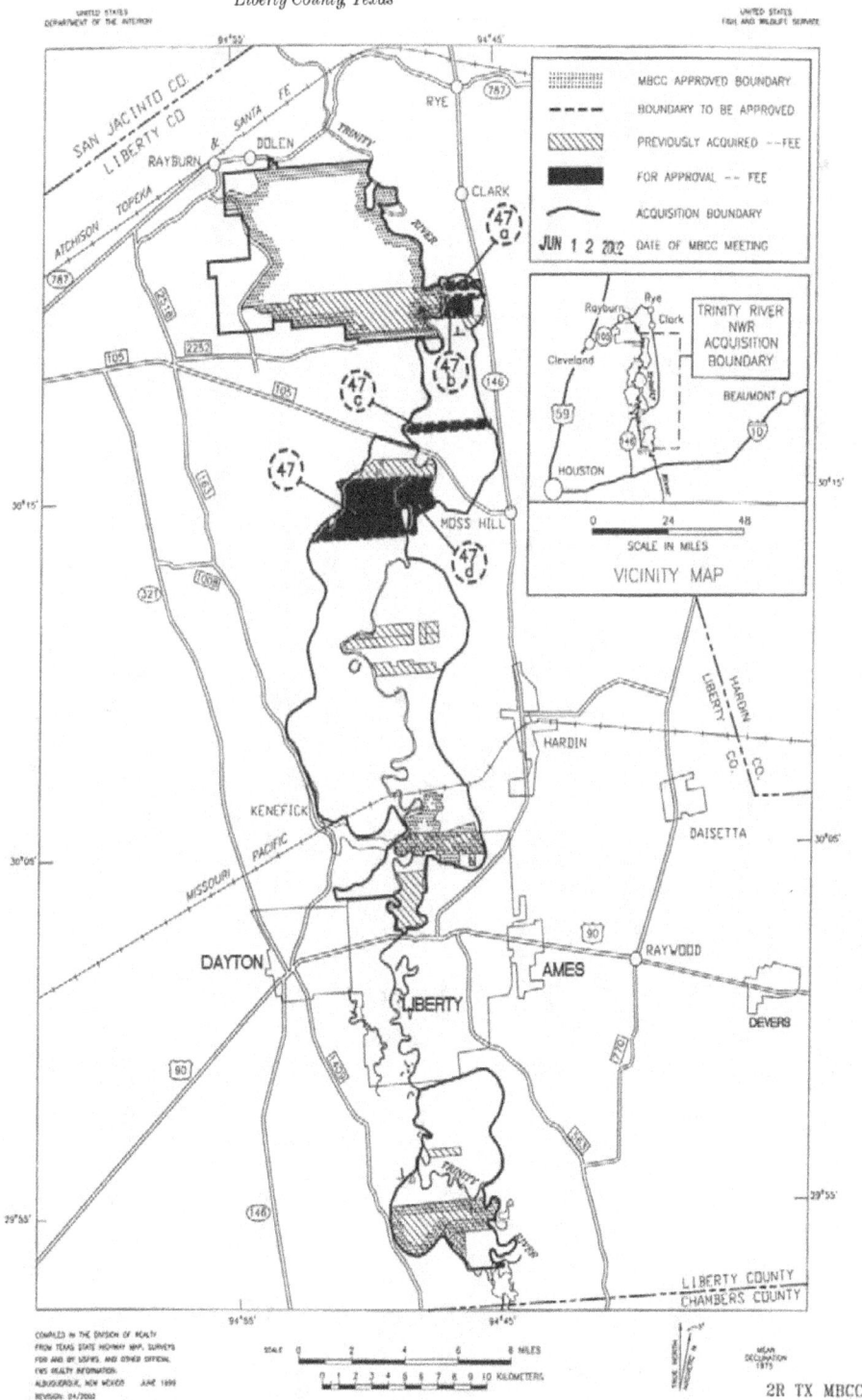

Membership of the National Migratory Bird Conservation Commission

Fiscal Year	Secretary of the Interior[2]	Secretary of Agriculture[2]	Secretary of Commerce[3]	Secretary of Transportation[4]	Administrator of Environmental Protection Agency[5]	Members on Part of the Senate		Members on Part of the House		Secretary to the Commission
1929	Roy L. Wilbur	Arthur M. Hyde	Robert P. Lamont			Harry B. Hawes	Peter Norbeck	Sam D. McReynolds	Ernest R. Ackerman	Rudolph Dieffenbach
1930										
1931			Roy D. Chapin							
1932			Daniel C. Roper			Key Pittman			August H. Andresen	
1933	Harold L. Ickes	Henry A. Wallace							Roy O. Woodruff	
1934									Chester C. Bolton	
1935										
1936							Charles L. McNary		James Wolfenden	
1937			Harry L. Hopkins			George L. Radcliffe				
1938								John J. Cochran		
1939										
1940			Jesse H. Jones							
1941		Claude R. Wickard								
1942										
1943									Walter E. Brehm	
1944							Vacant			
1945	Julius A. Krug	Clinton P. Anderson	Henry A. Wallace				C. Wayland Brooks	Frank M. Karsten		Arthur A. Riemer
1946										
1947			W. Averell Harriman							
1948		Charles F. Brannan	Charles W. Sawyer			A. Willis Robertson			August H. Andresen	
1949	Oscar L. Chapman					Raymond E. Baldwin				
1950						Vacant				
1951						John W. Bricker				
1952			Sinclair Weeks							
1953	Douglas McKay	Ezra Taft Benson								
1954										
1955						Thomas C. Hennings, Jr.				
1956	Fred A. Seaton								Leon H. Gavin	Albert J. Riseman
1957										
1958			Lewis L. Strauss				Roman L. Hruska			
1959			Frederick H. Mueller			Lee Metcalf				
1960			Luther H. Hodges							
1961	Stewart L. Udall	Orville L. Freeman								F. G. Spaden, Jr.
1962										
1963									George A. Gooding	
1964						Joseph O. Tydings	Henry L. Bellmon	John D. Dingell	Silvio O. Conte	
1965			John T. Connor			Lee Metcalf				
1966										
1967			Alexander B. Trowbridge	Alan S. Boyd						
1968										
1969	Walter J. Hickel	Clifford M. Hardin		John A. Volpe						
1970										Walter R. McAllester
1971	Rogers C. B. Morton	Earl L. Butz				Quentin N. Burdick				
1972										
1973				Claude S. Brinegar						
1974										
1975	Stanley K. Hathaway			William T. Coleman		Floyd K. Haskell				
1976	Thomas S. Kleppe									
1977	Cecil D. Andrus	Bob Bergland		Brock Adams						
1978						David H. Pryor				
1979				Neil Goldschmidt						
1980				Drew Lewis						
1981	James G. Watt	James R. Block								
1982										
1983	William P. Clark			Elizabeth H. Dole						
1984										
1985	Donald P. Hodel									
1986		Richard Lyng								
1987				James Burnley IV						
1988				Samuel K. Skinner						
1989	Manuel Lujan Jr.	Clayton Yeutter			William K. Reilly		Thad Cochran		Richard T. Schulze	William F. Hartwig
1990										
1991		Edward R. Madigan							Curt Weldon	
1992										
1993	Bruce Babbitt	Mike Espy			Carol M. Browner	John B. Breaux				Geoffrey L. Haskett
1994										
1995		Donald R. Glickman								
1996										
1997										
1998										
1999										
2000										
2001	Gale Norton	Ann M. Veneman			Christine Todd-Whitman					Jeffery M. Donahoe

[1] Chairman 1940 to date
[2] Chairman 1929 to 1939
[3] Member 1929 to March 1, 1968
[4] Member March 2, 1968 to December 12, 1989
[5] Member December 13, 1989 to date

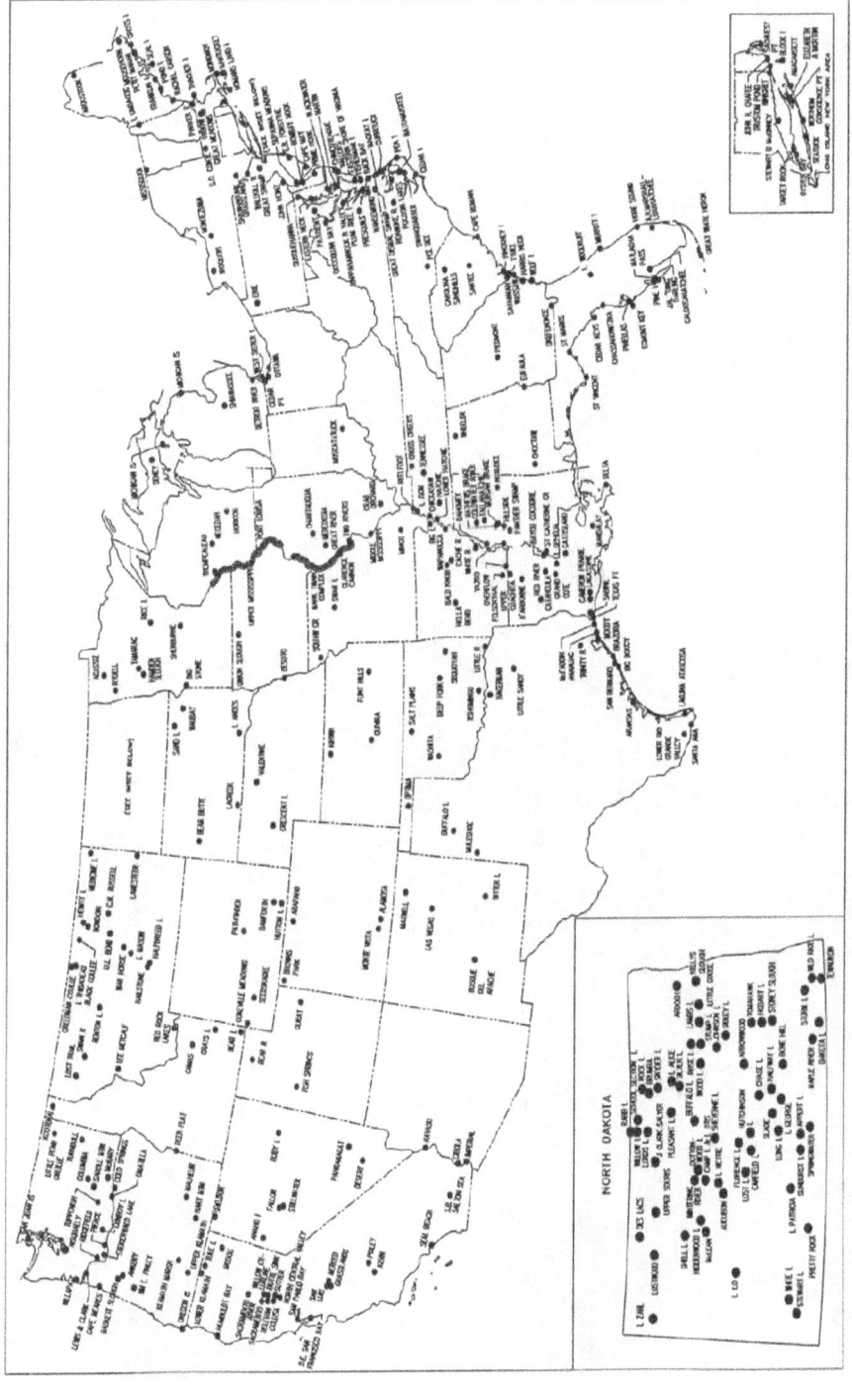

Migratory Bird Conservation Commission
National Migratory Bird Refuge Areas

UNITED STATES
DEPARTMENT OF THE INTERIOR

UNITED STATES
FISH AND WILDLIFE SERVICE

COMPILED IN THE DIVISION OF REALTY

WASHINGTON, DC   SEPTEMBER 30, 2002

Waterfowl Production Areas

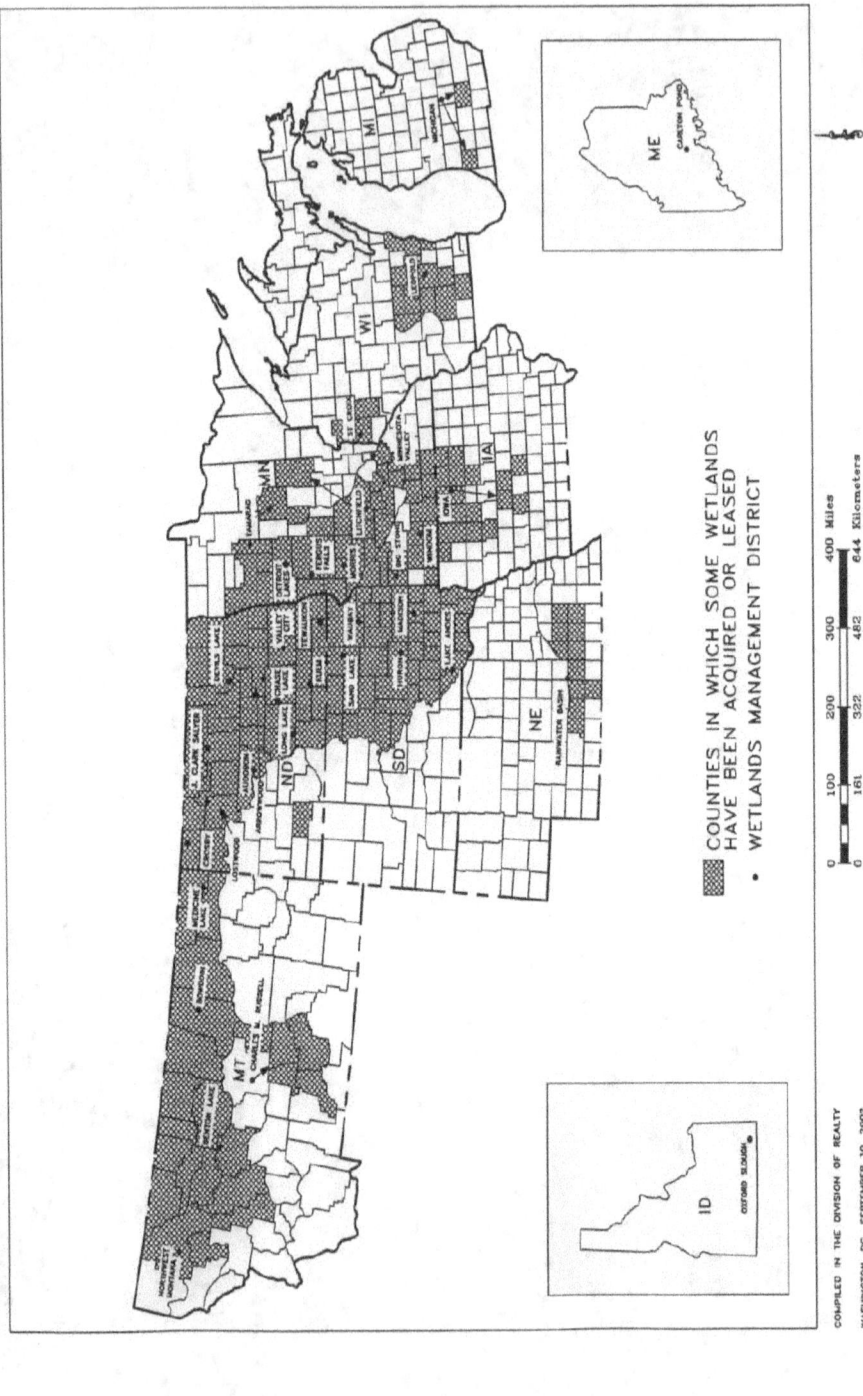

COUNTIES IN WHICH SOME WETLANDS
HAVE BEEN ACQUIRED OR LEASED

• WETLANDS MANAGEMENT DISTRICT

0	100	200	300	400 Miles
0	161	322	482	644 Kilometers

COMPILED IN THE DIVISION OF REALTY

WASHINGTON, DC SEPTEMBER 30, 2002

14

Notes on Tables One and Two

The information contained in this report includes those acquisitions and dispositions of land and interests therein that are purchased with Migratory Bird Conservation Fund monies or acquired under the authority of the Migratory Bird Conservation Act. It also includes other migratory bird areas such as those that are transferred to the Fish and Wildlife Service under the authority of Public Law 80-537 to carry out a migratory bird management program (these will appear on Table 1).

In an ongoing effort to improve data quality, the figures in Tables One and Two may show minor changes from previous annual reports. Lands in which the Service previously acquired a less- than-fee interest (leases and easements) may be purchased in fee during the year, and the number of easement or lease acres will show a decrease and the number of purchased acres an increase. The acreage appearing in the Approvals and Summary of Land Acquisitions sections of this report will not appear in Tables One or Two until after the tracts are acquired and the funds are actually expended. Also, a newly approved refuge will not appear on Table One until the tracts are acquired.

For information on all lands and interests under U.S. Fish and Wildlife Service control, refer to the "*Annual Report of Lands Under Control of the U.S. Fish and Wildlife Service.*" This report can be obtained from the U.S. Fish and Wildlife Service Division of Realty at http://realty. fws.gov or by calling 703/358 1713.

STATE AND UNIT	FISCAL YEAR MBCF ACQUISITION				CUMULATIVE TOTALS AT END OF FISCAL YEAR					
	PURCHASED		EASEMENT OR LEASE		MBCF				ALL OTHER	TOTAL
					PURCHASED		EASEMENT OR LEASE		ACRES	ACRES
	ACRES	COST	ACRES	COST	ACRES	COST	ACRES	COST		
ALABAMA										
CHOCTAW	0.00	0.00	0.00	0.00	0.00	0.00	0.00	0.00	4,218.00	4,218.00
EUFAULA (1)	0.00	0.00	0.00	0.00	0.00	0.00	0.00	0.00	7,958.19	7,958.19
FSA INTEREST AL ** *	0.00	0.00	0.00	0.00	0.00	0.00	0.00	0.00	742.69	742.69
WHEELER	0.00	0.00	0.00	0.00	50.70	0.00	0.00	0.00	34,379.96	34,430.66
TOTAL 3	0.00	0.00	0.00	0.00	50.70	0.00	0.00	0.00	47,298.84	47,344.54
ARIZONA										
CIBOLA (2)	0.00	0.00	0.00	0.00	0.00	0.00	0.00	0.00	8,606.04	8,606.04
HAVASU (2)	0.00	0.00	0.00	0.00	0.00	0.00	0.00	0.00	30,279.82	30,279.82
IMPERIAL (2)	0.00	0.00	0.00	0.00	0.00	0.00	0.00	0.00	17,809.76	17,809.76
TOTAL 3	0.00	0.00	0.00	0.00	0.00	0.00	0.00	0.00	56,695.62	56,695.62
ARKANSAS										
BALD KNOB	0.00	0.00	0.00	0.00	4,486.00	2,954,000.00	0.00	0.00	10,273.95	14,759.95
BIG LAKE	0.00	0.00	0.00	0.00	467.20	25,654.89	.25	2.00	10,568.65	11,036.10
CACHE RIVER	850.00	1,144,000.00	0.00	0.00	40,870.36	32,455,101.92	0.00	0.00	16,088.87	56,959.25
FELSENTHAL	0.00	0.00	0.00	0.00	0.00	0.00	0.00	0.00	64,902.14	64,902.14
FSA INTEREST AR ** *	0.00	0.00	0.00	0.00	0.00	0.00	0.00	0.00	3,458.67	3,458.67
HOLLA BEND	0.00	0.00	0.00	0.00	690.45	336,905.00	0.00	5,175.00	5,608.58	6,299.03
OVERFLOW	0.00	0.00	0.00	0.00	12,962.89	10,300,520.50	0.00	0.00	0.00	12,962.89
WAPANOCCA	0.00	0.00	0.00	0.00	5,484.17	1,351,416.00	0.00	0.00	0.00	5,484.17
WHITE RIVER	472.43	750,000.00	0.00	0.00	10,143.63	5,254,645.37	413.22	22.00	147,869.87	158,414.72
TOTAL 8	1,352.43	1,894,000.00	0.00	0.00	75,106.70	52,656,261.48	413.47	5,199.00	258,756.73	334,276.90
CALIFORNIA										
BUTTE SINK	0.00	0.00	0.00	0.00	514.98	1,650,700.00	10,310.64	12,816,903.00	217.86	11,043.50
CIBOLA (3) *	0.00	0.00	0.00	0.00	0.00	0.00	0.00	0.00	4,246.52	4,246.52
COLUSA	0.00	0.00	0.00	0.00	2,384.74	107,313.30	0.00	0.00	1,695.24	4,089.98
DELEVAN	0.00	0.00	0.00	0.00	5,796.54	2,345,739.00	0.00	175,000.00	0.00	5,796.54
DON EDWARDS SAN FRAN. BAY	0.00	0.00	0.00	0.00	0.00	0.00	0.00	0.00	22,389.74	22,389.74
FSA INTEREST CA ** *	0.00	0.00	0.00	0.00	0.00	0.00	0.00	0.00	80.00	80.00
GRASSLANDS	0.00	0.00	189.00	132,300.00	5,172.86	5,396,866.00	67,479.07	29,521,666.00	7,891.97	80,543.92
HAVASU (3) *	0.00	0.00	0.00	0.00	0.00	0.00	0.00	0.00	7,285.34	7,285.34
HUMBOLDT BAY	0.00	0.00	0.00	0.00	2,425.40	5,099,410.00	0.00	0.00	486.32	2,911.72
IMPERIAL (3) *	0.00	0.00	0.00	0.00	0.00	0.00	0.00	0.00	7,958.19	7,958.19
KERN	0.00	0.00	0.00	0.00	10,543.86	579,912.00	0.00	0.00	74.31	10,618.17
LOWER KLAMATH (4)	329.00	395,000.00	0.00	0.00	4,530.53	3,390,125.00	0.00	0.00	39,763.61	44,294.14
MERCED	0.00	0.00	0.00	0.00	3,803.82	2,180,000.00	0.00	0.00	1.76	3,805.58
MODOC	0.00	0.00	0.00	0.00	5,359.58	1,077,684.19	0.00	0.00	1,661.65	7,021.23
NORTH CENTRAL VALLEY	119.30	417,500.00	0.00	0.00	586.63	1,565,581.00	6,430.45	9,426,390.00	113.31	7,130.39
PIXLEY	0.00	0.00	0.00	0.00	0.00	0.00	0.00	0.00	6,389.13	6,389.13
SACRAMENTO	0.00	0.00	0.00	0.00	10,775.61	150,498.00	0.00	0.00	7.73	10,785.34
SACRAMENTO RIVER	0.00	0.00	0.00	0.00	0.00	0.00	0.00	0.00	17,520.30	17,520.30
SAN LUIS	0.00	0.00	0.00	0.00	7,422.41	2,171,055.00	705.00	2,284,000.00	14,768.00	22,895.41
SAN PABLO BAY	0.00	0.00	0.00	0.00	248.00	243,400.00	0.00	0.00	12,941.72	13,189.72
SEAL BEACH	0.00	0.00	0.00	0.00	0.00	0.00	0.00	0.00	910.71	910.71
SONNY BONO SALTON SEA	0.00	0.00	0.00	0.00	9,342.14	294,461.80	657.00	1,089.27	27,679.73	37,658.87
SUTTER	0.00	0.00	0.00	0.00	2,590.16	291,281.80	0.00	3,860.00	0.00	2,590.16
TULE LAKE	0.00	0.00	0.00	0.00	0.00	0.00	0.00	0.00	39,116.58	39,116.58

STATE AND UNIT		FISCAL YEAR MBCF ACQUISITION				CUMULATIVE TOTALS AT END OF FISCAL YEAR					
		PURCHASED		EASEMENT OR LEASE		MBCF				ALL OTHER	TOTAL
						PURCHASED		EASEMENT OR LEASE		ACRES	ACRES
		ACRES	COST	ACRES	COST	ACRES	COST	ACRES	COST		
CALIFORNIA											
WILLOW CREEK-LURLINE		0.00	0.00	0.00	0.00	0.00	0.00	5,467.50	6,686,683.00	0.00	5,467.50
TOTAL	21	448.30	812,500.00	189.00	132,300.00	71,495.28	26,543,955.09	91,027.66	60,715,531.27	213,121.74	375,644.68
COLORADO											
ALAMOSA		611.29	191,000.00	-611.29	0.00	10,266.42	1,590,463.16	0.00	24,055.90	902.69	11,169.11
ARAPAHO		0.00	0.00	0.00	0.00	17,811.33	4,798,286.00	0.00	35,359.66	5,432.54	23,243.87
BROWNS PARK		0.00	0.00	0.00	1,690.70	5,275.63	614,976.00	1,505.42	63,046.66	6,874.25	13,655.30
FSA INTEREST CO	** *	0.00	0.00	0.00	0.00	0.00	0.00	0.00	0.00	296.00	296.00
MONTE VISTA		0.00	0.00	0.00	0.00	13,950.66	2,241,750.00	0.00	0.00	853.33	14,803.99
TOTAL	4	611.29	191,000.00	(611.29)	1,690.70	47,304.04	9,245,475.16	1,505.42	122,442.22	14,598.81	62,998.27
CONNECTICUT											
STEWART B. MCKINNEY		0.00	0.00	0.00	0.00	361.24	2,263,560.00	0.00	0.00	511.10	872.34
TOTAL	1	0.00	0.00	0.00	0.00	361.24	2,263,560.00	0.00	0.00	511.10	872.34
DELAWARE											
BOMBAY HOOK		0.00	0.00	0.00	0.00	15,278.48	1,619,286.60	80.00	2.00	699.28	16,057.76
FSA INTEREST DE	** *	0.00	0.00	0.00	0.00	0.00	0.00	0.00	0.00	2.60	2.60
PRIME HOOK		0.00	0.00	0.00	0.00	8,276.67	3,620,266.18	95.49	5,346.20	1,693.93	10,066.09
TOTAL	2	0.00	0.00	0.00	0.00	23,555.15	5,239,556.76	175.49	5,348.20	2,395.81	26,126.45
FLORIDA											
ARTHUR R. MARSHALL		0.00	0.00	0.00	0.00	2,549.77	118,511.97	0.00	0.00	145,287.60	145,787.37
CALOOSAHATCHEE		0.00	0.00	0.00	0.00	0.00	0.00	0.00	0.00	40.00	40.00
CEDAR KEYS		0.00	0.00	0.00	0.00	0.00	0.00	0.00	0.00	891.15	891.15
CHASSAHOWITZKA		0.00	0.00	0.00	0.00	22,556.82	267,529.26	0.00	0.00	8,286.09	50,842.91
EGMONT KEY		0.00	0.00	0.00	0.00	0.00	0.00	0.00	0.00	528.30	528.30
FSA INTEREST FL	** *	0.00	0.00	0.00	0.00	0.00	0.00	0.00	0.00	3,125.93	3,125.93
GREAT WHITE HERON		0.00	0.00	0.00	0.00	1,326.54	906,195.00	0.00	0.00	191,461.09	192,787.63
HOBE SOUND		0.00	0.00	0.00	0.00	0.00	0.00	0.00	0.00	1,033.72	1,033.72
J. N. DING DARLING		0.00	0.00	0.00	0.00	541.98	572,570.00	0.00	0.00	5,846.30	6,388.28
LAKE WOODRUFF		0.00	0.00	0.00	0.00	18,413.39	1,340,310.75	0.00	0.00	3,145.63	21,559.02
MATLACHA PASS		0.00	0.00	0.00	0.00	0.00	0.00	0.00	0.00	392.64	392.64
MERRITT ISLAND		0.00	0.00	0.00	0.00	0.00	0.00	0.00	0.00	139,189.40	139,189.40
OKEEFENOKEE	(1)	0.00	0.00	0.00	0.00	0.00	0.00	0.00	0.00	5,724.48	5,724.48
PINE ISLAND		0.00	0.00	0.00	0.00	0.00	0.00	0.00	0.00	602.24	602.24
PINELLAS		0.00	0.00	0.00	0.00	0.00	0.00	0.00	0.00	394.33	394.33
ST. MARKS		0.00	0.00	0.00	0.00	30,985.17	102,311.61	116.72	0.00	31,246.29	62,348.18
ST. VINCENT		0.00	0.00	0.00	0.00	12,358.20	2,085,000.00	0.00	0.00	131.73	12,489.93
TOTAL	16	0.00	0.00	0.00	0.00	88,731.87	5,142,228.99	116.72	0.00	533,074.54	621,925.13
GEORGIA											
EUFAULA	(5) *	0.00	0.00	0.00	0.00	0.00	0.00	0.00	0.00	3,251.00	3,251.00
FSA INTEREST GA	** *	0.00	0.00	0.00	0.00	0.00	0.00	0.00	0.00	4,795.57	4,795.57
HARRIS NECK		0.00	0.00	0.00	0.00	0.00	0.00	0.00	0.00	2,828.92	2,828.92
OKEEFENOKEE	(6) *	0.00	0.00	0.00	0.00	343,208.94	867,318.12	0.00	0.00	46,198.05	391,401.99
PIEDMONT		0.00	0.00	0.00	0.00	473.97	44,000.00	0.00	0.00	34,493.01	34,966.98
SAVANNAH	(7)	0.00	0.00	0.00	0.00	8,027.84	1,705,352.40	0.00	0.00	5,295.64	13,325.48
WASSAW		0.00	0.00	0.00	0.00	0.00	0.00	0.00	0.00	10,069.87	10,069.87

STATE AND UNIT		FISCAL YEAR MBCF ACQUISITION				CUMULATIVE TOTALS AT END OF FISCAL YEAR					
		PURCHASED		EASEMENT OR LEASE		MBCF				ALL OTHER	TOTAL
						PURCHASED		EASEMENT OR LEASE		ACRES	ACRES
		ACRES	COST	ACRES	COST	ACRES	COST	ACRES	COST		
GEORGIA											
WOLF ISLAND		0.00	0.00	0.00	0.00	4,587.62	120,013.52	0.00	0.00	588.00	5,125.62
TOTAL	5	0.00	0.00	0.00	0.00	358,298.57	2,757,484.04	0.00	0.00	107,440.06	465,758.63
IDAHO											
BEAR LAKE		0.00	0.00	0.00	0.00	626.57	212,279.30	-.00	1.00	17,459.01	18,085.58
CAMAS		0.00	0.00	0.00	0.00	10,438.46	202,700.84	0.00	0.00	139.88	10,578.34
DEER FLAT	(4)	0.00	0.00	0.00	0.00	242.89	26,415.90	0.00	0.00	11,022.50	11,265.39
FSA INTEREST ID	** *	0.00	0.00	0.00	0.00	0.00	0.00	0.00	0.00	1,110.60	1,110.60
GRAYS LAKE		148.90	203,000.00	0.00	0.00	3,488.18	1,339,000.00	32.49	4,518.30	16,049.41	19,565.08
KOOTENAI		0.00	0.00	0.00	0.00	2,774.15	708,100.00	0.00	0.00	.14	2,774.29
TOTAL	5	148.90	203,000.00	0.00	0.00	17,565.25	2,488,495.64	32.49	4,519.30	45,781.54	63,579.28
ILLINOIS											
CHAUTAUQUA		0.00	0.00	0.00	0.00	44.54	2,525.38	0.00	0.00	6,401.03	6,445.57
CRAB ORCHARD		0.00	0.00	0.00	0.00	227.76	402,780.00	0.00	0.00	43,660.76	43,888.52
FSA INTEREST IL	** *	0.00	0.00	0.00	0.00	0.00	0.00	0.00	0.00	535.40	535.40
GREAT RIVER	(8)	0.00	0.00	0.00	0.00	1,559.87	353,202.72	0.00	0.00	5,550.76	7,110.63
MEREDOSIA		0.00	0.00	0.00	0.00	0.00	0.00	0.00	0.00	3,400.80	3,400.80
MIDDLE MISSISSIPPI RIVER	(8)	0.00	0.00	0.00	0.00	0.00	0.00	0.00	0.00	2,257.55	2,257.55
PORT LOUISA	(19)	0.00	0.00	0.00	0.00	0.00	0.00	0.00	0.00	1,470.89	1,470.89
TWO RIVERS	(8)	0.00	0.00	0.00	0.00	796.17	346,943.75	0.00	0.00	7,257.03	8,053.20
TOTAL	7	0.00	0.00	0.00	0.00	2,628.34	1,105,451.85	0.00	0.00	70,294.20	72,922.54
INDIANA											
FSA INTEREST IN	** *	0.00	0.00	0.00	0.00	0.00	0.00	0.00	0.00	219.03	219.03
MUSCATATUCK		0.00	0.00	0.00	0.00	7,715.53	3,582,887.72	0.00	0.00	86.69	7,802.22
TOTAL	1	0.00	0.00	0.00	0.00	7,715.53	3,582,887.72	0.00	0.00	305.72	8,021.25
IOWA											
DESOTO	(10)	0.00	0.00	0.00	0.00	3,444.79	657,117.53	0.00	0.00	57.98	3,502.77
PORT LOUISA	(11)*	0.00	0.00	0.00	0.00	47.50	16,000.00	0.00	6.00	22,575.87	22,623.37
UNION SLOUGH		0.00	0.00	0.00	0.00	2,845.24	210,407.69	70.70	608.00	0.00	2,915.94
TOTAL	2	0.00	0.00	0.00	0.00	6,337.53	863,525.22	70.70	608.00	22,633.85	29,042.08
KANSAS											
FLINT HILLS		0.00	0.00	0.00	0.00	0.00	0.00	0.00	0.00	18,463.36	18,463.36
FSA INTEREST KS	** *	0.00	0.00	0.00	0.00	0.00	0.00	0.00	0.00	116.50	116.50
KIRWIN		0.00	0.00	0.00	0.00	0.00	0.00	0.00	0.00	10,778.00	10,778.00
QUIVIRA		0.00	0.00	0.00	0.00	21,820.10	2,059,258.00	0.00	0.00	199.20	22,019.30
TOTAL	3	0.00	0.00	0.00	0.00	21,820.10	2,059,258.00	0.00	0.00	29,557.06	51,377.16
KENTUCKY											
REELFOOT	(14)	0.00	0.00	0.00	0.00	2,039.64	418,450.15	0.00	0.00	0.00	2,039.64
TOTAL	1	0.00	0.00	0.00	0.00	2,039.64	418,450.15	0.00	0.00	0.00	2,039.64
LOUISIANA											
BAYOU COCODRIE		0.00	0.00	0.00	0.00	3,563.60	2,016,578.00	0.00	0.00	9,804.91	13,168.51
CAMERON PRAIRIE		0.00	0.00	0.00	0.00	9,621.30	5,090,650.00	0.00	0.00	0.00	9,621.30
CAT ISLAND		0.00	0.00	0.00	0.00	632.00	500,000.00	0.00	0.00	1,722.91	2,354.91

ANNUAL REPORT OF THE MIGRATORY BIRD CONSERVATION COMMISSION
MIGRATORY BIRD CONSERVATION FUND ACQUISITIONS

TABLE ONE

NATIONAL MIGRATORY BIRD AREAS IN THE CONTERMINOUS UNITED STATES

STATE AND UNIT		FISCAL YEAR MBCF ACQUISITION				CUMULATIVE TOTALS AT END OF FISCAL YEAR					
		PURCHASED		EASEMENT OR LEASE		MBCF				ALL OTHER	TOTAL
						PURCHASED		EASEMENT OR LEASE			
		ACRES	COST	ACRES	COST	ACRES	COST	ACRES	COST	ACRES	ACRES
LOUISIANA											
CATAHOULA		0.00	0.00	0.00	0.00	14,789.86	2,130,082.25	0.00	0.00	119.75	14,909.61
D'ARBONNE		0.00	0.00	0.00	0.00	0.00	0.00	0.00	0.00	17,419.63	17,419.63
DELTA		0.00	0.00	0.00	0.00	34,462.73	233,324.17	0.00	0.00	14,336.37	48,799.10
FSA INTEREST LA	** *	0.00	0.00	0.00	0.00	0.00	0.00	0.00	0.00	14,025.95	14,025.95
GRAND COTE		0.00	0.00	0.00	0.00	0.00	479,173.00	0.00	0.00	6,077.00	6,077.00
LACASSINE		0.00	0.00	0.00	12,800.00	9,806.29	999,156.63	652.51	147,900.00	23,819.97	34,378.77
LAKE OPHELIA		29.60	107,500.00	0.00	0.00	3,058.60	1,429,990.00	0.00	0.00	14,496.56	17,555.16
MANDALAY		0.00	0.00	0.00	0.00	0.00	0.00	0.00	0.00	4,619.00	4,619.00
RED RIVER		1,377.14	1,000,000.00	0.00	0.00	1,377.14	1,000,000.00	0.00	0.00	2,480.00	3,857.14
SABINE		0.00	0.00	0.00	0.00	566.66	14,000.51	0.00	0.00	140,150.15	140,716.81
UPPER OUACHITA		1,352.95	2,849,325.00	0.00	0.00	41,958.98	20,596,986.00	3,265.88	525,760.00	641.00	45,660.81
TOTAL	13	2,759.69	3,956,825.00	0.00	12,800.00	119,712.16	34,489,880.36	3,918.34	673,660.00	249,733.20	373,363.70
MAINE											
AROOSTOOK		0.00	0.00	0.00	0.00	0.00	0.00	0.00	0.00	4,695.07	4,695.07
CROSS ISLAND		0.00	0.00	0.00	0.00	0.00	0.00	0.00	0.00	1,705.10	1,705.10
FRANKLIN ISLAND		0.00	0.00	0.00	0.00	0.00	0.00	0.00	0.00	11.94	11.94
FSA INTEREST ME	** *	0.00	0.00	0.00	0.00	0.00	0.00	0.00	0.00	622.06	622.06
LAKE UMBAGOG	(36) *	622.00	192,620.00	0.00	0.00	1,519.40	426,970.00	0.00	0.00	2,846.47	4,365.87
MOOSEHORN		2,699.00	1,137,416.35	0.00	0.00	18,682.40	1,706,874.19	6.49	2.00	8,991.56	27,680.45
PETIT MANAN		0.00	0.00	0.00	0.00	1,472.30	390,000.00	0.00	0.00	4,184.56	5,656.86
POND ISLAND		0.00	0.00	0.00	0.00	0.00	0.00	0.00	0.00	10.00	10.00
RACHEL CARSON		0.00	0.00	0.00	0.00	2,848.79	1,513,346.75	2.97	3,100.00	2,235.92	5,087.68
SEAL ISLAND		0.00	0.00	0.00	0.00	0.00	0.00	0.00	0.00	65.00	65.00
TOTAL	8	3,521.00	1,330,256.35	0.00	0.00	24,522.89	3,997,190.94	9.46	3,102.00	25,325.70	49,858.05
MARYLAND											
BLACKWATER		199.06	611,396.62	0.00	0.00	19,398.16	9,314,262.86	0.00	1.00	5,591.71	24,989.87
CHINCOTEAGUE	(16) *	0.00	0.00	0.00	0.00	417.81	18,780.42	0.00	0.00	0.00	417.81
EASTERN NECK		0.00	0.00	0.00	0.00	2,286.27	1,606,145.09	0.00	0.00	0.00	2,286.27
FSA INTEREST MD	** *	0.00	0.00	0.00	0.00	0.00	0.00	0.00	0.00	67.94	67.94
MARTIN	(16)	0.00	0.00	0.00	0.00	1,858.57	61,077.00	0.00	0.00	2,569.86	4,428.43
PATUXENT		0.00	0.00	0.00	0.00	431.95	7,667.57	0.00	0.00	12,409.27	12,841.20
SUSQUEHANNA		0.00	0.00	0.00	0.00	0.00	0.00	0.00	0.00	3.79	3.79
TOTAL	5	199.06	611,396.62	0.00	0.00	24,387.74	11,002,862.94	0.00	1.00	20,642.57	45,050.31
MASSACHUSETTS											
ASSABET RIVER		0.00	0.00	0.00	0.00	0.00	0.00	0.00	0.00	2,229.20	2,229.20
GREAT MEADOWS		2.40	9,600.00	0.00	0.00	2,819.54	1,864,518.90	0.00	0.00	892.05	3,711.59
MONOMOY		0.00	0.00	0.00	0.00	2,665.71	18,539.00	0.00	0.00	36.14	2,701.85
NANTUCKET		0.00	0.00	0.00	0.00	0.00	0.00	0.00	0.00	24.00	24.00
NOMANS LAND ISLAND		0.00	0.00	0.00	0.00	0.00	0.00	0.00	0.00	628.00	628.00
OXBOW		0.00	0.00	0.00	0.00	0.00	0.00	0.00	0.00	1,677.02	1,677.02
PARKER RIVER		0.00	0.00	0.00	0.00	4,686.29	107,740.84	0.00	0.00	14.22	4,652.51
SILVIO O. CONTE	(42) *	0.00	0.00	0.00	0.00	0.00	0.00	0.00	0.00	185.69	185.69
THACHER ISLAND		0.00	0.00	0.00	0.00	0.00	0.00	0.00	0.00	22.00	22.00
TOTAL	8	2.40	9,600.00	0.00	0.00	10,126.54	1,990,998.74	0.00	0.00	5,708.32	15,831.86

STATE AND UNIT		FISCAL YEAR MBCF ACQUISITION				CUMULATIVE TOTALS AT END OF FISCAL YEAR					
		PURCHASED		EASEMENT OR LEASE		MBCF				ALL OTHER	TOTAL
						PURCHASED		EASEMENT OR LEASE			
		ACRES	COST	ACRES	COST	ACRES	COST	ACRES	COST	ACRES	ACRES
MICHIGAN											
DETROIT RIVER		0.00	0.00	0.00	0.00	0.00	0.00	0.00	0.00	325.62	325.62
FSA INTEREST MI	** *	0.00	0.00	0.00	0.00	0.00	0.00	0.00	0.00	94.00	94.00
MICHIGAN ISLANDS		0.00	0.00	0.00	0.00	0.00	0.00	0.00	0.00	597.39	597.39
SENEY		0.00	0.00	0.00	0.00	74,914.90	127,726.66	0.00	0.00	20,329.91	95,244.81
SHIAWASSEE		-468.03	0.00	0.00	0.00	8,376.46	1,401,015.67	0.00	0.00	986.29	9,362.75
TOTAL	4	(468.03)	0.00	0.00	0.00	83,291.36	1,528,742.33	0.00	0.00	22,333.21	105,624.57
MINNESOTA											
AGASSIZ		0.00	0.00	0.00	0.00	822.11	40,226.04	0.00	0.00	60,678.82	61,500.93
BIG STONE		0.00	0.00	0.00	0.00	0.00	0.00	0.00	0.00	11,520.13	11,520.13
FSA INTEREST MN	** *	0.00	0.00	0.00	0.00	0.00	0.00	0.00	0.00	1,788.80	1,788.80
HAMDEN SLOUGH		0.00	0.00	0.00	0.00	3,111.29	1,787,872.00	73.40	0.00	9.16	3,193.85
RICE LAKE		0.00	0.00	0.00	0.00	6,435.60	197,529.77	0.00	0.00	10,036.68	16,472.28
RYDELL		0.00	0.00	0.00	0.00	0.00	0.00	0.00	0.00	2,070.00	2,070.00
SHERBURNE		-4.69	0.00	0.00	0.00	29,601.20	3,773,341.05	0.00	0.00	6.24	29,607.44
TAMARAC		0.00	0.00	0.00	0.00	35,151.38	612,159.93	0.00	0.00	40.00	35,191.38
TOTAL	7	(4.69)	0.00	0.00	0.00	75,121.58	5,910,928.79	73.40	0.00	86,144.88	161,339.81
MISSISSIPPI											
COLDWATER RIVER		306.60	368,000.00	0.00	0.00	2,374.10	1,430,450.00	0.00	0.00	94.26	2,468.36
DAHOMEY		0.00	0.00	0.00	2,600.00	0.00	0.00	260.00	20,800.00	8,906.80	9,166.80
FSA INTEREST MS	** *	0.00	0.00	0.00	0.00	0.00	0.00	0.00	0.00	28,696.09	28,696.09
HILLSIDE		373.27	522,600.00	0.00	0.00	3,644.02	2,877,600.00	0.00	0.00	15,407.37	19,051.39
MATHEWS BRAKE		0.00	0.00	0.00	0.00	2,418.74	1,691,446.00	0.00	0.00	0.00	2,418.74
MORGAN BRAKE		0.00	0.00	0.00	0.00	7,241.26	4,517,452.20	0.00	0.00	131.85	7,373.11
NOXUBEE		0.00	0.00	0.00	0.00	1,412.34	145,413.05	0.00	0.00	45,636.85	47,049.19
PANTHER SWAMP		0.00	0.00	0.00	16,032.00	27,956.19	14,990,725.00	640.00	60,982.00	7,075.66	35,271.85
ST. CATHERINE CREEK		0.00	0.00	0.00	5,525.10	24,429.29	12,925,167.00	502.10	28,639.82	0.00	24,931.39
TALLAHATCHIE		0.00	0.00	0.00	0.00	2,207.00	1,171,000.00	0.00	0.00	470.00	2,677.00
YAZOO		80.34	68,300.00	0.00	0.00	13,020.77	2,760,803.78	0.00	0.00	2.21	13,022.98
TOTAL	10	760.21	958,900.00	0.00	24,155.10	84,303.73	42,510,085.03	1,402.10	110,021.82	106,421.07	192,126.90
MISSOURI											
CLARENCE CANNON		0.00	0.00	0.00	0.00	3,736.04	1,163,649.25	0.00	0.00	13.94	3,749.98
FSA INTEREST MO	** *	0.00	0.00	0.00	0.00	0.00	0.00	0.00	0.00	1,784.68	1,784.68
GREAT RIVER	(11)*	0.00	0.00	0.00	0.00	1,119.78	460,000.00	0.00	0.00	988.15	2,107.93
MIDDLE MISSISSIPPI RIVER	(11)*	0.00	0.00	0.00	0.00	0.00	0.00	0.00	0.00	1,704.17	1,704.17
MINGO		0.00	0.00	0.00	0.00	21,620.76	298,615.82	11.86	27.00	113.24	21,745.86
SQUAW CREEK		0.00	0.00	0.00	0.00	801.32	38,275.46	1.00	0.00	6,612.57	7,414.89
SWAN LAKE		0.00	0.00	0.00	0.00	5,399.32	355,194.19	0.00	0.00	6,093.65	11,492.97
TWO RIVERS	(11)*	0.00	0.00	0.00	0.00	0.00	0.00	0.00	0.00	252.00	252.00
TOTAL	4	0.00	0.00	0.00	0.00	32,677.22	2,315,734.72	12.86	27.00	17,542.40	50,252.48
MONTANA											
BENTON LAKE		0.00	0.00	0.00	0.00	147.64	5,315.00	68.69	8,763.00	12,343.11	12,459.44
BLACK COULEE		0.00	0.00	0.00	0.00	0.00	0.00	0.00	0.00	1,308.86	1,308.86
BOWDOIN		0.00	0.00	0.00	0.00	0.00	0.00	0.00	0.00	15,551.97	15,551.97
CHARLES M. RUSSELL		0.00	0.00	0.00	0.00	0.00	0.00	0.00	0.00	912,348.32	912,348.32
CREEDMAN COULEE		0.00	0.00	0.00	0.00	0.00	0.00	0.00	0.00	2,728.00	2,728.00

STATE AND UNIT		FISCAL YEAR MBCF ACQUISITION				CUMULATIVE TOTALS AT END OF FISCAL YEAR					
		PURCHASED		EASEMENT OR LEASE		MBCF				ALL OTHER	TOTAL
						PURCHASED		EASEMENT OR LEASE			
		ACRES	COST	ACRES	COST	ACRES	COST	ACRES	COST	ACRES	ACRES
MONTANA											
FSA INTEREST MT	** *	0.00	0.00	0.00	0.00	0.00	0.00	0.00	0.00	510.62	510.62
HAILSTONE		0.00	0.00	0.00	0.00	0.00	0.00	0.00	0.00	920.00	920.00
HALFBREED LAKE		0.00	0.00	0.00	1,048.80	3,379.02	291,000.00	1,089.22	28,428.50	0.00	4,518.24
HEWITT LAKE		0.00	0.00	0.00	0.00	0.00	0.00	0.00	0.00	1,360.92	1,360.92
LAKE MASON		0.00	0.00	0.00	0.00	4,100.45	0.00	0.00	0.00	12,714.07	16,814.52
LAKE THIBADEAU		0.00	0.00	0.00	0.00	0.00	0.00	0.00	0.00	3,868.48	3,868.48
LAMESTEER		0.00	0.00	0.00	0.00	0.00	0.00	0.00	0.00	800.00	800.00
LEE METCALF		0.00	0.00	0.00	0.00	2,696.29	799,680.00	0.00	0.00	96.23	2,792.52
LOST TRAIL		0.00	0.00	0.00	869.52	4,695.20	1,728,205.00	1,029.04	2,447.70	3,112.00	8,824.24
MEDICINE LAKE		0.00	0.00	0.00	0.00	2,513.26	25,460.00	0.00	0.00	28,970.75	31,484.01
RED ROCK LAKES		0.00	0.00	0.00	0.00	1,024.75	70,109.00	0.00	0.00	50,719.66	51,744.41
SWAN RIVER		0.00	0.00	0.00	0.00	1,568.81	901,645.00	0.00	0.00	0.00	1,568.81
UL BEND		0.00	0.00	0.00	0.00	9,688.19	577,280.00	0.00	0.00	46,361.37	56,049.56
WAR HORSE		0.00	0.00	0.00	0.00	0.00	0.00	0.00	0.00	3,192.24	3,192.24
TOTAL	18	0.00	0.00	0.00	1,918.52	29,711.61	4,398,694.00	2,136.95	54,614.20	1,096,806.62	1,128,655.18
NEBRASKA											
CRESCENT LAKE		0.00	0.00	0.00	0.00	6,574.55	31,048.00	31.49	3,189.00	39,389.31	45,995.35
DESOTO	(19)*	0.00	0.00	0.00	0.00	3,640.52	591,507.20	0.00	0.00	665.88	4,324.20
FSA INTEREST NE	** *	0.00	0.00	0.00	0.00	0.00	0.00	0.00	0.00	2,092.72	2,092.72
VALENTINE		0.00	0.00	0.00	0.00	5,078.54	62,747.00	0.00	0.00	67,959.75	73,038.09
TOTAL	2	0.00	0.00	0.00	0.00	15,313.21	685,302.20	31.49	3,189.00	110,105.66	125,450.36
NEVADA											
ANAHO ISLAND		0.00	0.00	0.00	0.00	0.00	0.00	0.00	0.00	247.73	247.73
DESERT		0.00	0.00	0.00	0.00	320.00	5,600.00	0.00	0.00	1,585,498.55	1,585,818.55
FALLON		0.00	0.00	0.00	0.00	0.00	0.00	0.00	0.00	17,901.94	17,901.94
PAHRANAGAT		0.00	0.00	0.00	0.00	3,915.60	500,000.00	.75	0.00	1,466.39	5,382.74
RUBY LAKE		0.00	0.00	0.00	0.00	29,945.73	208,437.25	0.00	0.00	9,340.37	39,286.10
SHELDON	(4)	0.00	0.00	0.00	0.00	23,143.67	2,032.00	0.00	0.00	549,732.48	572,876.15
STILLWATER		0.00	0.00	0.00	0.00	0.00	0.00	0.00	0.00	86,884.94	86,884.94
TOTAL	7	0.00	0.00	0.00	0.00	57,325.00	716,069.25	.75	0.00	2,254,082.40	2,311,408.15
NEW HAMPSHIRE											
LAKE UMBAGOG	(37)	2,928.63	1,528,275.00	0.00	0.00	4,400.59	2,128,275.00	0.00	0.00	7,783.38	12,183.97
SILVIO O. CONTE	(43)*	0.00	0.00	0.00	0.00	0.00	0.00	0.00	0.00	670.82	670.82
TOTAL	1	2,928.63	1,528,275.00	0.00	0.00	4,400.59	2,128,275.00	0.00	0.00	8,454.20	12,854.79
NEW JERSEY											
CAPE MAY		118.18	161,400.00	0.00	0.00	4,951.22	4,928,843.00	0.00	0.00	6,359.16	10,910.38
EDWIN B. FORSYTHE		41.77	42,000.00	0.00	0.00	38,714.09	15,415,995.83	0.00	1,300.00	6,477.04	45,191.13
GREAT SWAMP		0.00	0.00	0.00	0.00	2,956.43	3,977,691.05	1.27	1.00	4,573.25	7,530.95
SUPAWNA MEADOWS		0.00	0.00	0.00	0.00	2,526.83	968,744.00	0.00	0.00	367.92	2,894.75
WALLKILL RIVER	(39)*	0.00	0.00	0.00	0.00	1,138.89	2,294,665.00	0.00	0.00	3,520.72	4,669.61
TOTAL	4	159.95	203,400.00	0.00	0.00	49,897.46	27,185,958.88	1.27	1,301.00	21,308.09	71,196.82
NEW MEXICO											
BITTER LAKE		0.00	0.00	0.00	0.00	10,953.66	52,304.00	0.00	0.00	13,654.98	24,608.64
BOSQUE DEL APACHE		0.00	0.00	0.00	0.00	56,850.31	125,311.00	0.00	0.00	340.79	57,191.10

21

STATE AND UNIT		FISCAL YEAR MBCF ACQUISITION				CUMULATIVE TOTALS AT END OF FISCAL YEAR					
		PURCHASED		EASEMENT OR LEASE		MBCF				ALL OTHER	TOTAL
						PURCHASED		EASEMENT OR LEASE		ACRES	ACRES
		ACRES	COST	ACRES	COST	ACRES	COST	ACRES	COST		
NEW MEXICO											
LAS VEGAS		0.00	0.00	0.00	0.00	8,672.08	2,121,150.00	0.00	0.00	0.00	8,672.08
MAXWELL		0.00	0.00	0.00	0.00	2,791.69	423,570.79	0.00	0.00	906.90	3,698.59
TOTAL	4	0.00	0.00	0.00	0.00	79,267.74	2,722,185.79	0.00	0.00	14,902.67	94,170.41
NEW YORK											
AMAGANSETT		0.00	0.00	0.00	0.00	0.00	0.00	0.00	0.00	35.84	35.84
CONSCIENCE POINT		0.00	0.00	0.00	0.00	0.00	0.00	0.00	0.00	60.40	60.40
ELIZABETH A. MORTON		0.00	0.00	0.00	0.00	0.00	0.00	0.00	0.00	187.19	187.19
FSA INTEREST NY	** *	0.00	0.00	0.00	0.00	0.00	0.00	0.00	0.00	2,714.10	2,714.10
IROQUOIS		0.00	0.00	0.00	0.00	10,757.81	1,279,615.46	0.00	0.00	70.25	10,828.06
MONTEZUMA		50.00	25,000.00	0.00	0.00	7,510.72	2,014,906.56	13.15	4.00	933.17	8,457.04
OYSTER BAY		0.00	0.00	0.00	0.00	0.00	0.00	0.00	0.00	3,204.06	3,204.06
SEATUCK		0.00	0.00	0.00	0.00	0.00	0.00	0.00	0.00	209.23	209.23
SHAWANGUNK GRASSLANDS		0.00	0.00	0.00	0.00	0.00	0.00	0.00	0.00	566.58	566.58
TARGET ROCK		0.00	0.00	0.00	0.00	0.00	0.00	0.00	0.00	80.09	80.09
WALLKILL RIVER	(40)	0.00	0.00	0.00	0.00	0.00	0.00	0.00	0.00	147.09	147.09
WERTHEIM		0.00	0.00	0.00	0.00	188.70	195,217.80	0.00	0.00	2,380.66	2,569.36
TOTAL	11	50.00	25,000.00	0.00	0.00	18,457.23	3,487,739.82	13.15	4.00	10,588.63	29,059.01
NORTH CAROLINA											
CEDAR ISLAND		0.00	0.00	0.00	0.00	12,484.77	347,171.21	0.00	0.00	1,997.55	14,482.52
CURRITUCK		0.00	0.00	0.00	0.00	3,479.79	6,362,098.00	225.76	120,000.00	4,324.09	8,029.64
FSA INTEREST NC	** *	0.00	0.00	0.00	0.00	0.00	0.00	0.00	0.00	6,434.04	6,434.04
GREAT DISMAL SWAMP	(16)	1,297.90	1,112,180.00	0.00	0.00	1,297.90	1,112,180.00	0.00	0.00	24,811.80	26,109.70
MACKAY ISLAND	(16)	0.00	0.00	0.00	0.00	6,528.15	865,906.95	0.00	0.00	935.19	7,463.34
MATTAMUSKEET		0.00	0.00	0.00	0.00	252.04	1,285.35	0.00	0.00	49,928.14	50,180.18
PEA ISLAND		0.00	0.00	0.00	0.00	5,787.97	40,401.86	0.00	0.00	46.23	5,834.20
PEE DEE		0.00	0.00	0.00	0.00	8,438.94	2,561,881.76	0.00	0.00	0.00	8,438.94
POCOSIN LAKES		0.00	0.00	0.00	0.00	12,350.35	1,682,157.99	0.00	0.00	97,756.19	110,106.54
ROANOKE RIVER		0.00	0.00	0.00	0.00	13,106.63	6,345,258.00	0.00	0.00	4,870.00	17,976.63
SWANQUARTER		0.00	0.00	0.00	0.00	15,492.76	60,920.98	0.00	0.00	918.93	16,411.69
TOTAL	10	1,297.90	1,112,180.00	0.00	0.00	79,019.30	19,379,232.05	225.76	120,000.00	192,021.56	271,266.62
NORTH DAKOTA											
APPERT LAKE		0.00	0.00	0.00	0.00	0.00	0.00	0.00	0.00	907.75	907.75
ARDOCH		0.00	0.00	0.00	0.00	288.13	2,739.00	0.00	0.00	2,408.00	2,696.13
ARROWWOOD		0.00	0.00	0.00	0.00	2,097.51	46,906.58	0.00	0.00	13,845.35	15,942.86
AUDUBON		0.00	0.00	0.00	0.00	0.00	0.00	0.00	0.00	14,739.19	14,739.19
BONE HILL		0.00	0.00	0.00	0.00	0.00	0.00	0.00	0.00	640.00	640.00
BRUMBA		0.00	0.00	0.00	0.00	0.00	0.00	0.00	0.00	1,977.48	1,977.48
BUFFALO LAKE		0.00	0.00	0.00	0.00	0.00	0.00	0.00	0.00	1,568.72	1,568.72
CAMP LAKE		0.00	0.00	0.00	0.00	0.00	0.00	0.00	0.00	584.70	584.70
CANFIELD LAKE		0.00	0.00	0.00	0.00	3.10	100.00	0.00	0.00	310.13	313.23
CHASE LAKE		0.00	0.00	0.00	0.00	4,449.47	25,611.00	0.00	0.00	0.00	4,449.47
COTTONWOOD LAKE		0.00	0.00	0.00	0.00	0.00	0.00	0.00	0.00	1,013.47	1,013.47
DAKOTA LAKE		0.00	0.00	0.00	0.00	0.00	0.00	0.00	0.00	2,799.78	2,799.78
DES LACS		0.00	0.00	0.00	0.00	701.82	6,895.60	2.70	0.00	18,842.62	19,547.14
FLORENCE LAKE		0.00	0.00	0.00	0.00	1,466.40	31,405.00	0.00	0.00	419.80	1,886.20
FSA INTEREST ND	** *	0.00	0.00	0.00	0.00	0.00	0.00	0.00	0.00	6,591.40	6,591.40

ANNUAL REPORT OF THE MIGRATORY BIRD CONSERVATION COMMISSION
MIGRATORY BIRD CONSERVATION FUND ACQUISITIONS

TABLE ONE

NATIONAL MIGRATORY BIRD AREAS IN THE CONTERMINOUS UNITED STATES

STATE AND UNIT		FISCAL YEAR MBCF ACQUISITION				CUMULATIVE TOTALS AT END OF FISCAL YEAR					
		PURCHASED		EASEMENT OR LEASE		MBCF				ALL OTHER	TOTAL
						PURCHASED		EASEMENT OR LEASE		ACRES	ACRES
		ACRES	COST	ACRES	COST	ACRES	COST	ACRES	COST		
RHODE ISLAND											
TOTAL	5	0.00	0.00	0.00	0.00	0.00	0.00	0.00	0.00	2,179.21	2,179.21
SOUTH CAROLINA											
CAPE ROMAIN		0.00	0.00	0.00	0.00	22,257.29	17,218.18	0.00	0.00	42,987.65	65,224.94
CAROLINA SANDHILLS		0.00	0.00	0.00	0.00	580.20	38,352.75	0.00	0.00	44,768.23	45,348.43
FSA INTEREST SC	** *	0.00	0.00	0.00	0.00	0.00	0.00	0.00	0.00	1,430.04	1,430.04
PINCKNEY ISLAND		0.00	0.00	0.00	0.00	0.00	0.00	0.00	0.00	4,052.70	4,052.70
SANTEE		0.00	0.00	0.00	0.00	4,322.43	549,993.57	0.00	0.00	8,160.85	12,483.28
SAVANNAH	(1) *	0.00	0.00	0.00	0.00	7,401.37	1,350,490.30	0.00	0.00	7,471.08	14,872.45
TYBEE		0.00	0.00	0.00	0.00	0.00	0.00	0.00	0.00	100.00	100.00
TOTAL	5	0.00	0.00	0.00	0.00	34,541.29	1,956,014.80	0.00	0.00	108,970.55	143,511.84
SOUTH DAKOTA											
BEAR BUTTE		0.00	0.00	0.00	0.00	0.00	0.00	0.00	0.00	374.20	374.20
FSA INTEREST SD	** *	0.00	0.00	0.00	0.00	0.00	0.00	0.00	0.00	151.20	151.20
LACREEK		0.00	0.00	0.00	0.00	9,579.75	788,491.00	445.00	15,938.00	7,030.58	16,055.33
LAKE ANDES		0.00	0.00	0.00	0.00	617.64	92,322.00	0.00	0.00	5,021.79	5,639.43
SAND LAKE		0.00	0.00	0.00	0.00	3,917.39	90,622.00	320.37	3.00	17,582.43	21,820.19
WAUBAY		0.00	0.00	0.00	0.00	688.77	28,888.00	90.53	0.00	3,965.92	4,740.22
TOTAL	5	0.00	0.00	0.00	0.00	14,568.55	995,273.00	855.90	15,941.00	34,126.12	49,580.57
TENNESSEE											
CHICKASAW		273.66	370,000.00	0.00	0.00	14,331.24	15,504,764.00	0.00	0.00	9,008.47	23,339.71
CROSS CREEKS		0.00	0.00	0.00	0.00	87.64	26,200.00	0.00	0.00	8,773.85	8,861.49
FSA INTEREST TN	** *	0.00	0.00	0.00	0.00	0.00	0.00	0.00	0.00	685.39	685.39
HATCHIE		0.00	0.00	0.00	0.00	11,220.73	1,862,329.25	0.00	0.00	335.37	11,556.10
LAKE ISOM		0.00	0.00	0.00	0.00	344.65	27,290.72	0.00	0.00	1,501.31	1,845.96
LOWER HATCHIE		161.33	306,900.00	0.00	0.00	8,492.48	11,163,126.00	0.00	0.00	2,343.89	10,836.37
REELFOOT	(22) *	0.00	0.00	0.00	0.00	496.53	109,531.78	0.00	0.00	7,914.21	8,410.74
TENNESSEE		0.00	0.00	0.00	0.00	430.45	72,151.10	0.00	0.00	50,929.01	51,359.46
TOTAL	6	434.99	676,900.00	0.00	0.00	35,403.72	28,765,392.85	0.00	0.00	81,491.50	116,895.22
TEXAS											
ANAHUAC		0.00	0.00	0.00	0.00	29,924.59	12,440,198.40	63.09	0.00	4,308.75	34,296.23
ARANSAS		0.00	0.00	0.00	0.00	49,255.68	1,833,531.80	24,895.00	0.00	40,269.40	114,412.08
BIG BOGGY		0.00	0.00	0.00	0.00	4,118.41	2,374,594.19	258.23	58,112.00	154.53	4,526.17
BRAZORIA		0.00	0.00	0.00	0.00	42,641.25	15,822,482.26	0.00	0.00	1,772.65	44,413.88
BUFFALO LAKE		0.00	0.00	0.00	0.00	0.00	0.00	0.00	0.00	7,664.16	7,664.16
FSA INTEREST TX	** *	0.00	0.00	0.00	0.00	0.00	0.00	0.00	0.00	1,878.13	1,878.13
HAGERMAN		0.00	0.00	0.00	0.00	0.00	0.00	0.00	0.00	11,319.84	11,319.84
LAGUNA ATASCOSA		0.00	0.00	0.00	0.00	56,497.13	6,206,915.89	0.00	0.00	8,599.10	65,096.23
LITTLE SANDY		0.00	0.00	0.00	0.00	0.00	0.00	3,802.00	0.00	0.00	3,802.00
MCFADDIN		0.00	0.00	0.00	0.00	48,431.82	10,219,500.00	7,748.88	1,394,170.00	0.00	56,180.70
MOODY		0.00	0.00	0.00	0.00	0.00	0.00	3,516.87	0.00	0.00	3,516.87
MULESHOE		0.00	0.00	0.00	0.00	2,154.80	25,740.00	0.00	0.00	3,654.30	5,809.10
SAN BERNARD		0.00	0.00	0.00	0.00	27,527.91	7,708,314.94	0.00	0.00	6,128.63	33,656.54
SANTA ANA		0.00	0.00	0.00	0.00	1,980.50	25,766.00	.52	0.00	106.48	2,087.50
TEXAS POINT		0.00	0.00	0.00	0.00	8,952.02	1,719,000.00	0.00	0.00	0.00	8,952.02
TRINITY RIVER		1,295.06	660,570.00	0.00	0.00	4,325.75	2,199,070.00	0.00	0.00	8,594.33	12,920.08

STATE AND UNIT		FISCAL YEAR MBCF ACQUISITION				CUMULATIVE TOTALS AT END OF FISCAL YEAR					
		PURCHASED		EASEMENT OR LEASE		MBCF				ALL OTHER ACRES	TOTAL ACRES
						PURCHASED		EASEMENT OR LEASE			
		ACRES	COST	ACRES	COST	ACRES	COST	ACRES	COST		
TEXAS											
TOTAL	15	1,299.06	660,570.00	0.00	0.00	275,784.64	58,572,868.48	40,282.99	1,452,282.00	94,464.30	410,531.53
UTAH											
BEAR RIVER		0.00	0.00	0.00	5.00	25,772.64	2,864,119.47	46.64	740.00	47,826.10	73,645.38
FISH SPRINGS		0.00	0.00	0.00	0.00	3,774.82	98,525.00	0.00	75.00	14,217.42	17,992.24
FSA INTEREST UT	** *	0.00	0.00	0.00	0.00	0.00	0.00	0.00	0.00	280.84	280.84
OURAY		0.00	0.00	0.00	13,891.00	5,014.98	487,884.25	3,964.68	300,227.92	3,278.58	12,258.24
TOTAL	3	0.00	0.00	0.00	13,896.00	34,562.44	3,464,528.72	4,011.32	301,040.92	65,602.94	104,176.70
VERMONT											
FSA INTEREST VT	** *	0.00	0.00	0.00	0.00	0.00	0.00	0.00	0.00	71.00	71.00
MISSISQUOI		0.00	0.00	0.00	0.00	6,155.14	291,154.27	0.00	0.00	366.34	6,521.48
SILVIO O. CONTE	(41)	244.31	61,500.00	0.00	0.00	17,112.31	4,278,574.00	0.00	0.00	9421.80	26,534.11
TOTAL	1	244.31	61,500.00	0.00	0.00	23,267.45	4,569,708.27	0.00	0.00	9,859.14	33,126.59
VIRGINIA											
BACK BAY		0.00	0.00	0.00	0.00	7,389.62	4,868,182.00	0.00	0.00	1,413.30	8,802.92
CHINCOTEAGUE	(25)	0.00	0.00	0.00	0.00	9,513.02	685,425.91	0.00	0.00	4,101.43	13,614.45
EASTERN SHORE OF VIRGINIA		375.80	1,058,000.00	0.00	0.00	375.80	1,058,000.00	0.00	0.00	747.47	1,123.27
FISHERMAN ISLAND		0.00	0.00	0.00	0.00	825.00	1,600,000.00	0.00	0.00	1,124.50	1,949.50
FSA INTEREST VA	** *	0.00	0.00	0.00	0.00	0.00	0.00	0.00	0.00	133.70	133.70
GREAT DISMAL SWAMP	(24)*	0.00	0.00	0.00	0.00	2,896.42	2,824,762.98	0.00	0.00	82,196.69	85,093.11
MACKAY ISLAND	(24)*	0.00	0.00	0.00	0.00	874.40	26,859.75	0.00	0.00	0.00	874.40
MARTIN	(25)*	0.00	0.00	0.00	0.00	0.00	0.00	0.00	0.00	145.62	145.62
NANSEMOND		0.00	0.00	0.00	0.00	0.00	0.00	0.00	0.00	422.99	422.99
OCCOQUAN BAY		0.00	0.00	0.00	0.00	0.00	0.00	0.00	0.00	642.07	642.07
PLUM TREE ISLAND		0.00	0.00	0.00	0.00	0.00	0.00	0.00	0.00	3,501.68	3,501.68
PRESQUILE		0.00	0.00	0.00	0.00	0.00	0.00	0.00	0.00	1,328.92	1,328.92
RAPPAHANNOCK RIVER		0.00	0.00	0.00	0.00	280.00	672,000.00	0.00	0.00	4,456.31	4,736.31
WALLOPS ISLAND		0.00	0.00	0.00	0.00	0.00	0.00	0.00	0.00	3,373.00	3,373.00
TOTAL	10	375.80	1,058,000.00	0.00	0.00	22,154.26	11,685,204.64	0.00	0.00	103,587.68	125,741.94
WASHINGTON											
COLUMBIA		0.00	0.00	0.00	0.00	11,361.77	426,346.04	0.00	0.00	18,234.50	29,596.27
CONBOY LAKE		331.00	1,088,500.00	0.00	0.00	5,904.96	2,019,100.00	718.29	400,000.00	281.60	6,904.85
FSA INTEREST WA	** *	0.00	0.00	0.00	0.00	0.00	0.00	0.00	0.00	958.98	958.98
LITTLE PEND OREILLE		0.00	0.00	0.00	0.00	4,216.65	27,414.00	0.00	0.00	38,376.92	42,593.57
MCNARY		0.00	0.00	0.00	0.00	185.16	865.00	0.00	0.00	15,340.54	15,525.70
NISQUALLY		0.00	0.00	0.00	0.00	2,461.26	3,647,467.37	.55	3,000.00	1,258.02	3,719.83
PIERCE		0.00	0.00	0.00	0.00	0.00	0.00	0.00	0.00	329.58	329.58
RIDGEFIELD		0.00	0.00	0.00	0.00	4,670.16	4,033,600.00	1.74	21.00	545.80	5,217.70
SADDLE MOUNTAIN		0.00	0.00	0.00	0.00	0.00	0.00	0.00	0.00	161,485.95	161,485.95
SAN JUAN ISLANDS		0.00	0.00	0.00	0.00	0.00	0.00	0.00	0.00	448.53	448.53
TOPPENISH		0.00	0.00	0.00	0.00	1,762.80	599,157.00	1.29	0.00	214.75	1,978.84
TURNBULL		0.00	0.00	0.00	0.00	13,829.32	395,411.38	0.00	0.00	3,982.75	17,812.07
UMATILLA	(4) *	0.00	0.00	0.00	0.00	0.00	0.00	0.00	0.00	14,875.88	14,875.88
WILLAPA		0.00	0.00	0.00	0.00	8,616.42	5,122,010.74	.12	0.00	6,897.71	15,514.25
TOTAL	12	331.00	1,088,500.00	0.00	0.00	53,008.50	16,251,351.53	721.99	403,021.00	263,211.24	316,941.73

STATE AND UNIT		FISCAL YEAR MBCF ACQUISITION				CUMULATIVE TOTALS AT END OF FISCAL YEAR						
		PURCHASED		EASEMENT OR LEASE		MBCF				ALL OTHER	TOTAL
						PURCHASED		EASEMENT OR LEASE		ACRES	ACRES
		ACRES	COST	ACRES	COST	ACRES	COST	ACRES	COST		
WEST VIRGINIA											
FSA INTEREST WV	** *	0.00	0.00	0.00	0.00	0.00	0.00	0.00	0.00	8.57	8.57
TOTAL	0	0.00	0.00	0.00	0.00	0.00	0.00	0.00	0.00	8.57	8.57
WISCONSIN											
FSA INTEREST WI	** *	0.00	0.00	0.00	0.00	0.00	0.00	0.00	0.00	920.00	920.00
HORICON		0.00	0.00	0.00	0.00	20,874.90	473,257.42	29.00	356.00	277.95	21,181.85
NECEDAH		0.00	0.00	0.00	0.00	244.92	3,194.26	0.00	0.00	43,450.94	43,695.86
TREMPEALEAU		0.00	0.00	0.00	0.00	0.00	0.00	0.00	0.00	6,198.85	6,198.68
TOTAL	3	0.00	0.00	0.00	0.00	21,119.82	476,451.68	29.00	356.00	50,847.72	71,996.54
WYOMING											
BAMFORTH		0.00	0.00	0.00	0.00	964.80	6,368.00	0.00	0.00	201.23	1,166.03
COKEVILLE MEADOWS		0.00	0.00	520.00	4,167.68	4,738.89	2,101,412.61	320.00	4,167.68	3,528.43	8,587.32
FSA INTEREST WY	** *	0.00	0.00	0.00	0.00	0.00	0.00	0.00	0.00	3,132.75	3,132.75
HUTTON LAKE		0.00	0.00	0.00	0.00	1,815.49	7,943.00	0.00	0.00	152.85	1,968.34
PATHFINDER		0.00	0.00	0.00	0.00	0.00	0.00	0.00	0.00	16,806.90	16,806.90
SEEDSKADEE		0.00	0.00	0.00	0.00	0.00	0.00	0.00	0.00	27,230.22	27,230.22
TOTAL	5	0.00	0.00	320.00	4,167.68	7,519.18	2,115,723.61	320.00	4,167.68	51,052.58	58,891.56
GRAND TOTAL	354	16,760.20	16,902,382.97	(102.29)	190,927.80	2,272,627.98	434,588,260.40	151,330.26	63,976,402.61	7,256,191.32	9,659,711.82

(1) Also in GEORGIA
(2) * * CALIFORNIA
(3) * * ARIZONA
(4) * * OREGON
(5) * * ALABAMA
(6) * * FLORIDA
(7) * * SOUTH CAROLINA
(8) * * MISSOURI
(9) * * IOWA, MINNESOTA AND WISCONSIN
(10) * * NEBRASKA
(11) * * ILLINOIS
(12) * * TEXAS
(13) * * ILLINOIS, MINNESOTA AND WISCONSIN
(14) * * TENNESSEE
(15) * * NEVADA
(16) * * VIRGINIA
(17) * * NEW MEXICO
(18) * * ILLINOIS, IOWA AND WISCONSIN
(19) * * IOWA
(20) * * SOUTH DAKOTA
(21) * * IDAHO
(22) * * KENTUCKY
(23) * * MARYLAND
(24) * * NORTH CAROLINA
(25) * * ILLINOIS, IOWA AND MINNESOTA
(26) * * WASHINGTON
(27) * * MISSISSIPPI
(28) * * LOUISIANA
(34) * * WEST VIRGINIA AND KENTUCKY
(35) * * PENNSYLVANIA AND KENTUCKY
(36) * * NEW HAMPSHIRE
(37) * * MAINE
(38) * * WEST VIRGINIA AND PENNSYLVANIA
(39) * * NEW YORK
(40) * * NEW JERSEY
(41) * * MASSACHUSETTS AND NEW HAMPSHIRE
(42) * * VERMONT AND NEW HAMPSHIRE
(43) * * MASSACHUSETTS AND VERMONT
* - COUNTED IN ANOTHER STATE
** - DENOTES INTERESTS TRANSFERRED BY THE FSA
FSA - FARM SERVICE AGENCY (FORMERLY FARMERS HOME ADMINISTRATION, DEPARTMENT OF AGRICULTURE)

STATE AND UNIT	FISCAL YEAR MBCF ACQUISITION				CUMULATIVE TOTALS AT END OF FISCAL YEAR					
	PURCHASED		EASEMENT OR LEASE		MBCF				ALL OTHER	TOTAL
					PURCHASED		EASEMENT OR LEASE		ACRES	ACRES
	ACRES	COST	ACRES	COST	ACRES	COST	ACRES	COST		
IDAHO										
OXFORD SLOUGH	0.00	0.00	0.00	0.00	1,878.41	520,000.00	0.00	0.00	0.00	1,878.41
TOTAL 1	0.00	0.00	0.00	0.00	1,878.41	520,000.00	0.00	0.00	0.00	1,878.41
IOWA										
BOONE	0.00	0.00	0.00	0.00	391.33	599,600.00	0.00	0.00	0.00	391.33
BUENA VISTA	0.00	0.00	0.00	0.00	69.09	169,000.00	0.00	0.00	0.00	69.09
CERRO GORDO	0.00	0.00	0.00	0.00	2,494.25	2,882,677.82	5.70	10,200.00	0.00	2,499.95
CLAY	0.00	0.00	0.00	0.00	709.19	852,206.85	0.00	0.00	0.00	709.19
DICKINSON	210.00	386,650.00	0.00	0.00	4,261.13	5,080,516.00	98.00	37,725.00	635.34	4,994.47
EMMET	159.93	307,000.00	0.00	0.00	1,445.85	1,895,075.00	16.00	40,000.00	249.99	1,711.84
GREENE	155.00	420,000.00	0.00	0.00	669.05	1,260,700.00	0.00	0.00	0.00	669.05
GUTHRIE	0.00	0.00	0.00	0.00	185.93	295,840.00	0.00	0.00	0.00	185.93
HANCOCK	0.00	0.00	0.00	0.00	802.70	545,480.26	7.00	2,250.00	0.00	809.70
KOSSUTH	400.00	942,000.00	0.00	0.00	1,876.15	3,169,738.25	23.00	28,775.00	137.50	2,036.65
OSCEOLA	0.00	0.00	0.00	0.00	0.00	0.00	37.00	17,250.00	4.00	41.00
PALO ALTO	0.00	0.00	0.00	0.00	627.56	844,092.65	224.00	222,890.00	58.00	909.56
POCAHONTAS	0.00	0.00	0.00	0.00	225.76	455,000.00	0.00	0.00	0.00	225.76
POLK	0.00	0.00	0.00	0.00	110.00	261,500.00	0.00	0.00	0.00	110.00
SAC	0.00	0.00	0.00	0.00	296.52	363,080.00	0.00	0.00	0.00	296.52
WINNEBAGO	200.00	400,000.00	0.00	0.00	1,023.15	1,138,300.31	105.00	54,025.00	0.00	1,128.15
WORTH	0.00	0.00	0.00	0.00	1,491.84	1,008,329.67	18.00	9,250.00	0.00	1,509.84
WRIGHT	292.94	625,000.00	0.00	0.00	1,538.09	2,238,025.00	0.00	0.00	0.00	1,538.09
TOTAL 18	1,417.47	2,980,650.00	0.00	0.00	18,205.19	23,007,961.99	533.70	422,325.00	1,084.83	19,823.72
MAINE										
CARLTON POND	0.00	0.00	0.00	0.00	1,068.21	18,776.08	0.00	0.00	0.00	1,068.21
TOTAL 1	0.00	0.00	0.00	0.00	1,068.21	18,776.08	0.00	0.00	0.00	1,068.21
MICHIGAN										
JACKSON	0.00	0.00	0.00	0.00	160.00	170,000.00	0.00	0.00	0.00	160.00
VAN BUREN	0.00	0.00	0.00	0.00	77.08	43,600.00	0.00	0.00	0.00	77.08
TOTAL 2	0.00	0.00	0.00	0.00	237.08	213,600.00	0.00	0.00	0.00	237.08
MINNESOTA										
AITKIN	0.00	0.00	0.00	0.00	69.86	28,000.00	0.00	0.00	0.00	69.86
BECKER	0.00	0.00	228.73	137,300.00	11,756.70	3,162,020.56	2,012.14	533,335.10	10.81	13,779.65
BIG STONE	594.25	146,275.00	379.34	175,159.60	11,502.69	2,294,645.83	8,065.43	1,516,201.16	0.00	19,568.12
BLUE EARTH	0.00	0.00	0.00	0.00	868.45	1,222,900.00	78.70	141,575.00	58.48	1,025.63
CARVER	0.00	0.00	0.00	0.00	0.00	0.00	47.57	68,976.50	219.00	266.57
CASS	0.00	0.00	0.00	0.00	0.00	0.00	0.00	0.00	43.00	43.00
CHIPPEWA	0.00	0.00	17.40	12,100.00	244.10	127,050.00	57.00	32,900.00	0.00	301.10
CLAY	0.00	0.00	10.00	7,900.00	10,385.89	2,979,545.18	3,338.42	772,797.15	0.00	13,724.31
CLEARWATER	0.00	0.00	0.00	0.00	0.00	0.00	864.00	129,075.00	0.00	864.00
COTTONWOOD	0.00	0.00	.54	1,000.00	2,945.14	1,380,053.85	192.85	107,375.00	0.00	3,137.99
DAKOTA	0.00	0.00	0.00	0.00	73.90	201,747.00	0.00	0.00	.05	73.95
DOUGLAS	0.00	0.00	99.00	41,300.00	9,125.07	1,763,515.20	6,128.24	959,880.98	420.00	15,733.31
FARIBAULT	20.66	25,000.00	0.00	0.00	820.06	800,991.80	129.37	110,775.00	0.00	959.43
FREEBORN	0.00	0.00	0.00	0.00	1,631.99	1,883,367.25	143.26	145,625.00	0.00	1,775.25
GRANT	0.00	0.00	66.00	98,900.00	9,885.77	2,609,508.12	3,607.10	1,313,004.00	165.06	13,657.93

STATE AND UNIT	FISCAL YEAR MBCF ACQUISITION				CUMULATIVE TOTALS AT END OF FISCAL YEAR					
	PURCHASED		EASEMENT OR LEASE		MBCF				ALL OTHER	TOTAL
					PURCHASED		EASEMENT OR LEASE			
	ACRES	COST	ACRES	COST	ACRES	COST	ACRES	COST	ACRES	ACRES
MINNESOTA										
JACKSON	0.00	0.00	122.80	221,500.00	4,169.56	2,835,810.28	388.09	547,400.00	0.00	4,552.65
KANDIYOHI	1.30	1,600.00	0.00	0.00	13,224.08	4,980,725.93	4,264.03	562,451.00	1.68	17,491.39
LAC QUI PARLE	0.00	0.00	100.70	51,950.00	3,728.79	903,439.73	1,657.07	652,741.00	278.63	5,664.49
LESUEUR	0.00	0.00	0.00	0.00	350.91	438,754.50	209.15	126,728.50	62.88	622.94
LINCOLN	0.00	0.00	124.45	41,794.00	754.26	428,650.00	517.37	202,396.04	0.00	1,271.63
LYON	0.00	0.00	0.00	0.00	1,553.56	1,269,720.00	280.80	134,495.00	0.00	1,834.36
MAHNOMEN	0.00	0.00	0.00	0.00	5,399.33	863,558.90	4,947.00	161,511.00	0.00	10,346.33
MARTIN	0.00	0.00	0.00	0.00	70.89	45,369.60	271.65	287,184.39	0.00	342.54
MCLEOD	0.00	0.00	0.00	0.00	951.66	1,136,795.00	739.27	456,944.90	0.00	1,690.93
MEEKER	59.52	74,400.00	2.25	3,000.00	4,708.99	3,972,224.10	2,258.14	928,342.00	0.00	6,967.13
MURRAY	0.00	0.00	0.00	0.00	1,281.18	1,305,977.00	21.00	44,300.00	640.00	1,942.18
NOBLES	0.00	0.00	0.00	0.00	521.65	590,802.00	26.00	15,600.00	0.00	547.65
NORMAN	0.00	0.00	0.00	0.00	1,120.00	400,000.00	0.00	0.00	0.00	1,120.00
OTTER TAIL	8.25	12,375.00	295.50	121,900.00	20,814.98	6,879,052.26	14,026.43	3,032,455.25	92.29	34,933.10
POLK	0.00	0.00	0.00	0.00	11,537.35	2,169,752.86	1,743.80	263,925.00	0.00	13,281.15
POPE	0.00	0.00	138.00	64,650.00	12,755.79	2,396,265.07	8,913.08	1,056,152.20	208.32	21,877.19
RENVILLE	40.00	66,300.00	0.00	0.00	1,133.05	1,396,342.00	0.00	0.00	0.00	1,133.05
RICE	0.00	0.00	0.00	0.00	319.60	438,999.35	370.74	469,441.25	94.50	782.04
ROCK	0.00	0.00	0.00	0.00	0.00	0.00	11.00	9,350.00	0.00	11.00
SCOTT	0.00	0.00	0.00	0.00	40.00	109,200.00	164.21	248,001.00	0.00	204.21
SIBLEY	156.31	276,981.52	0.00	0.00	798.52	1,027,681.32	253.25	173,190.00	112.36	1,159.13
STEARNS	0.00	0.00	0.00	0.00	9,069.71	2,710,733.87	1,312.83	506,926.70	204.00	10,586.04
STEELE	170.00	60,000.00	0.00	0.00	630.11	653,244.00	0.00	0.00	0.00	630.11
STEVENS	-7.00	0.00	27.00	17,650.00	9,561.71	3,447,001.64	1,206.00	338,815.00	35.22	10,802.93
SWIFT	0.00	0.00	0.00	0.00	7,601.12	1,804,950.17	1,844.87	694,819.40	0.00	9,445.99
TODD	0.00	0.00	0.00	0.00	802.85	385,672.20	16.00	7,680.00	0.00	818.85
TRAVERSE	0.00	0.00	0.00	0.00	4,105.55	1,469,586.63	1,284.45	198,325.00	0.00	5,390.00
WASECA	248.78	408,000.00	0.00	0.00	248.78	408,000.00	0.00	0.00	0.00	248.78
WATONWAN	0.00	0.00	0.00	0.00	56.65	31,157.50	168.42	112,209.80	0.00	225.07
WILKIN	0.00	0.00	0.00	0.00	2,196.43	702,564.35	309.00	93,750.00	0.00	2,505.43
WRIGHT	0.00	0.00	0.00	0.00	2,500.92	2,527,820.90	437.50	229,575.00	0.00	2,938.42
YELLOW MEDICINE	0.00	0.00	0.00	0.00	959.58	703,685.30	235.09	98,027.40	0.00	1,194.67
TOTAL 47	1,292.07	1,068,931.32	1,609.71	957,105.60	182,298.36	66,791,887.25	72,585.62	17,471,997.52	2,708.28	257,542.26
MONTANA										
BLAINE	0.00	0.00	0.00	0.00	2,455.26	167,340.00	2,604.20	179,350.00	0.00	5,059.46
CASCADE	0.00	0.00	0.00	0.00	727.46	299,606.00	78.00	15,550.00	0.00	805.46
CHOUTEAU	0.00	0.00	0.00	1,541.00	2,136.13	588,543.00	501.00	19,326.00	0.00	2,637.13
DANIELS	0.00	0.00	0.00	0.00	1,080.58	97,669.00	472.65	41,125.00	546.52	2,099.75
FLATHEAD	0.00	0.00	0.00	0.00	4,410.31	2,246,518.00	0.00	0.00	807.92	5,218.23
GLACIER	0.00	0.00	0.00	0.00	94.20	17,896.00	9,721.83	919,045.00	96.50	9,912.53
GOLDEN VALLEY	0.00	0.00	0.00	187.68	760.27	76,427.00	160.00	4,974.61	0.00	920.27
HILL	0.00	0.00	0.00	851.00	0.00	0.00	918.00	80,021.00	378.93	1,296.93
LAKE	110.00	297,000.00	12.00	0.00	1,480.86	1,460,555.00	4,144.05	3,103,480.00	1,787.14	7,414.05
LEWIS AND CLARK	0.00	0.00	0.00	0.00	0.00	0.00	1,525.50	424,100.00	320.00	1,845.50
LIBERTY	0.00	0.00	0.00	0.00	0.00	0.00	428.00	14,100.00	0.00	428.00
MUSSELSHELL	0.00	0.00	0.00	720.00	532.45	165,001.00	160.00	5,915.00	0.00	692.45
PETROLEUM	0.00	0.00	0.00	0.00	40.00	25,800.00	0.00	0.00	0.00	40.00
PHILLIPS	0.00	0.00	550.64	130,458.16	6,528.83	1,206,863.00	23,613.05	1,608,412.12	559.50	30,701.38

STATE AND UNIT		FISCAL YEAR MBCF ACQUISITION				CUMULATIVE TOTALS AT END OF FISCAL YEAR					
						MBCF				ALL OTHER	TOTAL
		PURCHASED		EASEMENT OR LEASE		PURCHASED		EASEMENT OR LEASE			
		ACRES	COST	ACRES	COST	ACRES	COST	ACRES	COST	ACRES	ACRES
MONTANA											
PONDERA		0.00	0.00	4,936.25	1,186,600.00	640.00	95,000.00	8,487.01	1,760,000.00	0.00	9,127.01
POWELL		0.00	0.00	0.00	0.00	1,419.60	458,084.00	22,444.06	6,205,635.00	3,191.42	27,055.06
ROOSEVELT		0.00	0.00	0.00	0.00	179.20	14,000.00	7,402.42	392,500.00	0.00	7,581.62
SHERIDAN		0.00	0.00	0.00	0.00	9,348.01	950,442.25	9,703.70	679,255.00	1,710.13	20,761.84
STILLWATER		0.00	0.00	0.00	0.00	1,828.10	207,625.00	0.00	0.00	.38	1,828.48
TETON	*	0.00	0.00	0.00	0.00	1,486.05	376,253.00	4,964.42	70,500.00	136.04	6,586.51
TOOLE		0.00	0.00	0.00	0.00	4,329.18	985,964.00	12,161.09	914,265.00	5.28	16,495.55
VALLEY		0.00	0.00	0.00	0.00	0.00	0.00	201.00	28,160.00	0.00	201.00
YELLOWSTONE		0.00	0.00	0.00	0.00	486.42	55,600.00	0.00	0.00	0.00	486.42
TOTAL	25	110.00	297,000.00	5,498.92	1,320,357.84	39,742.91	9,437,186.25	109,891.98	16,473,643.75	9,589.76	159,174.65
NEBRASKA											
ADAMS		0.00	0.00	0.00	1,786.98	160.00	110,000.00	160.00	11,316.89	234.56	554.56
CLAY		0.00	0.00	0.00	0.00	4,496.27	1,622,444.00	0.00	0.00	1,868.31	6,364.58
FILLMORE		0.00	0.00	0.00	0.00	2,937.60	1,142,453.00	6.60	24.00	400.00	3,344.20
FRANKLIN		0.00	0.00	0.00	0.00	1,625.96	402,698.00	0.00	0.00	157.36	1,783.32
GOSPER		0.00	0.00	0.00	0.00	1,451.50	233,925.00	0.00	0.00	0.00	1,451.50
HALL	*	0.00	0.00	0.00	0.00	328.77	433,000.00	0.00	0.00	320.70	649.47
HAMILTON	*	0.00	0.00	0.00	0.00	400.00	407,450.00	0.00	5,899.02	726.00	1,126.00
KEARNEY	*	0.00	0.00	0.00	0.00	2,874.43	657,681.00	0.00	0.00	175.50	3,049.93
PHELPS		0.00	0.00	0.00	0.00	4,195.14	3,052,111.00	0.00	0.00	400.00	4,595.14
POLK FSA	** *	0.00	0.00	0.00	0.00	0.00	0.00	0.00	0.00	140.78	140.78
SALINE FSA	** *	0.00	0.00	0.00	0.00	0.00	0.00	0.00	0.00	104.35	104.35
SEWARD		0.00	0.00	0.00	0.00	283.38	101,746.45	0.00	0.00	187.76	471.14
YORK	*	0.00	0.00	0.00	0.00	679.20	194,429.00	0.00	0.00	241.00	920.20
TOTAL	11	0.00	0.00	0.00	1,788.98	19,432.25	8,357,995.45	166.60	17,299.91	4,956.32	24,555.17
NORTH DAKOTA											
BARNES	*	0.00	0.00	0.00	0.00	6,661.68	998,087.00	17,296.00	770,735.00	2,059.20	26,016.88
BENSON	*	0.00	0.00	0.00	0.00	7,322.66	607,908.00	35,530.00	987,455.00	4,837.67	47,690.33
BOTTINEAU	*	0.00	0.00	329.00	77,075.00	2,334.06	200,763.00	28,798.84	1,265,506.00	864.41	31,997.31
BURKE		0.00	0.00	184.00	42,725.00	3,544.19	180,068.00	26,028.00	598,680.00	15,259.58	44,851.77
BURLEIGH		0.00	0.00	0.00	0.00	9,451.44	1,899,164.00	25,087.00	513,700.00	7,246.75	41,785.19
CASS		0.00	0.00	0.00	0.00	3,424.81	623,044.00	1,709.00	133,825.00	50.90	5,184.71
CAVALIER		0.00	0.00	0.00	0.00	10,129.12	1,354,471.00	13,950.00	290,540.00	1,083.71	24,762.83
DICKEY		0.00	0.00	0.00	0.00	9,735.40	1,150,816.00	26,208.80	914,776.00	12,070.29	48,014.49
DIVIDE		0.00	0.00	0.00	0.00	9,444.62	474,790.00	34,574.09	646,705.00	1,317.83	45,336.54
EDDY	*	0.00	0.00	0.00	0.00	4,627.21	498,001.00	11,810.63	314,995.00	446.34	16,884.18
EMMONS	*	0.00	0.00	0.00	0.00	3,135.29	174,321.75	11,692.00	262,750.00	788.60	15,415.89
FOSTER		0.00	0.00	0.00	0.00	1,457.07	96,568.00	6,848.00	200,465.00	0.00	8,315.07
GRAND FORKS		625.02	536,760.00	0.00	0.00	5,981.90	1,213,522.05	1,118.00	46,485.00	641.26	7,741.26
GRIGGS		0.00	0.00	0.00	0.00	3,069.46	373,990.00	16,677.00	556,880.00	223.05	19,969.51
HETTINGER		0.00	0.00	0.00	0.00	0.00	0.00	0.00	0.00	1,202.60	1,202.60
KIDDER	*	0.00	0.00	0.00	0.00	5,633.00	438,429.00	63,229.00	964,500.00	5,875.80	74,738.68
LA MOURE	*	0.00	0.00	0.00	0.00	4,799.96	505,095.00	13,121.40	509,969.00	1,590.19	19,511.93
LOGAN	*	0.00	0.00	272.00	21,600.00	11,226.24	1,006,598.00	36,111.60	695,186.00	5,170.54	52,508.38
MCHENRY	*	0.00	0.00	1,743.00	108,275.00	4,888.80	374,404.50	27,798.00	805,170.00	16,319.49	49,006.29
MCINTOSH	*	0.00	0.00	50.00	2,700.00	17,373.48	1,368,865.00	29,761.00	709,000.00	570.08	47,704.56
MCLEAN		0.00	0.00	181.00	17,475.00	4,068.29	420,284.00	21,152.00	1,244,590.00	12,064.82	57,285.11

STATE AND UNIT		FISCAL YEAR MBCF ACQUISITION				CUMULATIVE TOTALS AT END OF FISCAL YEAR					
		PURCHASED		EASEMENT OR LEASE		MBCF				ALL OTHER	TOTAL
						PURCHASED		EASEMENT OR LEASE			
		ACRES	COST	ACRES	COST	ACRES	COST	ACRES	COST	ACRES	ACRES
NORTH DAKOTA											
MOUNTRAIL	*	0.00	0.00	728.00	102,125.00	10,195.10	940,661.00	29,619.40	763,580.00	14,326.22	54,100.72
NELSON	*	0.00	0.00	0.00	0.00	3,205.25	174,341.00	37,883.20	1,336,446.60	779.91	41,866.34
PEMBINA	*	0.00	0.00	0.00	0.00	2,258.56	218,678.00	139.00	1,900.00	252.30	2,649.86
PIERCE	*	0.00	0.00	0.00	0.00	8,437.74	922,095.00	36,246.00	1,162,285.00	9,716.37	54,570.11
RAMSEY	*	0.00	0.00	0.00	0.00	8,225.00	1,144,232.00	28,730.00	821,885.00	1,637.58	30,592.50
RANSOM		0.00	0.00	0.00	0.00	4,315.02	617,357.00	20,111.00	1,433,675.00	3,083.06	27,509.08
RENVILLE		0.00	0.00	358.00	124,875.00	311.09	23,523.00	15,381.00	1,352,266.00	22.60	15,714.69
RICHLAND		0.00	0.00	68.00	20,265.00	5,992.25	958,052.00	1,927.80	349,220.00	4,029.00	11,949.05
ROLETTE		0.00	0.00	0.00	0.00	5,694.08	759,347.00	19,898.01	429,420.00	722.96	26,310.00
SARGENT	*	0.00	0.00	107.00	52,500.00	3,537.46	305,439.00	14,219.00	846,036.00	7,191.79	24,948.25
SHERIDAN	*	0.00	0.00	951.00	100,325.00	7,661.50	468,427.00	30,164.39	982,795.00	15,418.88	53,244.77
STEELE		0.00	0.00	0.00	0.00	3,249.25	538,345.00	4,045.00	274,820.00	358.30	7,632.55
STUTSMAN		0.00	0.00	15.00	1,350.00	23,447.91	1,308,016.00	41,555.70	958,542.00	15,448.80	80,452.41
TOWNER		0.00	0.00	0.00	0.00	3,037.02	494,146.00	24,338.00	485,990.00	2,310.94	30,485.96
TRAILL		0.00	0.00	0.00	0.00	719.25	75,109.00	234.00	4,880.00	0.00	953.25
WALSH	*	0.00	0.00	0.00	0.00	1,393.19	98,125.00	8,758.40	118,801.00	731.23	10,882.82
WARD		0.00	0.00	742.00	96,050.00	5,668.09	489,211.00	38,728.61	1,308,964.00	4,673.37	49,270.07
WELLS	*	0.00	0.00	101.00	9,800.00	7,471.61	1,153,059.00	13,242.00	606,552.00	3,473.62	24,187.23
WILLIAMS	*	0.00	0.00	0.00	0.00	4,163.17	278,057.00	8,298.00	214,100.00	606.00	13,067.17
TOTAL	40	625.02	336,760.00	5,837.00	757,140.00	238,250.11	24,865,352.30	821,393.87	25,921,499.00	174,445.99	1,254,089.97
SOUTH DAKOTA				*							
AURORA	*	0.00	0.00	1,144.00	258,095.00	4,716.08	622,316.00	29,800.48	2,952,695.00	498.90	34,512.46
BEADLE	*	620.65	378,596.50	1,979.00	498,215.00	7,236.45	1,651,212.69	33,095.15	3,228,810.00	1,635.70	41,987.30
BON HOMME	*	0.00	0.00	0.00	0.00	1,174.17	323,624.90	159.00	4,305.00	93.73	1,426.90
BROOKINGS	*	0.00	0.00	44.00	9,575.00	6,051.85	1,430,276.70	6,256.25	1,182,876.00	1,235.50	13,543.63
BROWN		0.00	0.00	2,048.88	499,365.00	4,094.93	819,223.80	47,711.90	5,784,811.00	1,295.39	53,102.22
BRULE		0.00	0.00	1,932.84	414,530.00	1,074.13	89,404.00	16,727.26	1,104,465.00	889.43	18,640.82
BUFFALO		0.00	0.00	0.00	0.00	0.00	0.00	1,523.61	48,000.00	0.00	1,523.61
CAMPBELL		0.00	0.00	529.00	59,380.00	1,919.71	185,541.00	21,117.71	1,462,480.00	395.00	23,432.42
CHARLES MIX	*	0.00	0.00	539.56	112,410.00	4,098.15	1,142,147.00	6,499.19	509,885.00	1,167.81	11,765.15
CLARK	*	0.00	0.00	827.60	92,175.00	5,873.11	814,505.90	43,928.52	2,507,475.00	1,013.23	50,814.86
CLAY	*	0.00	0.00	0.00	0.00	40.00	8,000.00	7.00	200.00	52.50	99.50
CODINGTON		0.00	0.00	42.00	10,755.00	5,089.31	862,897.70	9,816.45	683,275.00	1,456.65	16,362.41
CORSON FSA	** *	0.00	0.00	0.00	0.00	0.00	0.00	0.00	0.00	1,105.90	1,105.90
DAVISON	*	5.40	1,620.00	0.00	0.00	229.92	24,540.00	179.00	14,365.00	175.10	584.02
DAY		0.00	0.00	725.56	66,900.00	6,332.63	457,107.00	43,497.81	2,855,470.00	1,599.32	51,429.76
DEUEL		75.58	64,250.00	243.00	36,400.00	3,186.37	459,022.00	20,702.35	1,555,800.00	1,603.48	25,492.20
DEWEY FSA	** *	0.00	0.00	0.00	0.00	0.00	0.00	0.00	0.00	956.80	956.80
DOUGLAS	*	0.00	0.00	0.00	0.00	3,852.05	647,691.00	3,187.17	181,965.00	713.17	7,752.39
EDMUNDS	*	0.00	0.00	3,742.87	406,000.00	8,965.76	1,717,201.00	113,336.69	7,666,700.00	983.80	123,286.25
FAULK	*	0.00	0.00	3,464.06	557,725.00	2,566.88	480,995.00	123,511.22	7,282,357.00	1,425.40	127,503.50
GRANT		0.00	0.00	863.78	108,800.00	5,362.99	1,005,000.00	15,254.87	878,090.00	0.00	20,617.86
HAAKON FSA	** *	0.00	0.00	0.00	0.00	0.00	0.00	0.00	0.00	1,806.10	1,806.10
HAMLIN	*	0.00	0.00	131.80	14,810.00	3,375.89	943,988.00	6,020.24	1,006,305.00	328.90	9,720.03
HAND		0.00	0.00	4,295.06	622,230.00	3,671.31	580,260.35	45,266.35	2,929,010.00	1,730.30	50,687.96
HANSON	*	243.00	198,000.00	2.00	1,000.00	1,075.60	281,853.00	2,600.48	136,150.00	132.00	3,805.08
HUGHES		0.00	0.00	297.50	27,500.00	455.99	82,800.00	744.50	48,825.00	0.00	1,200.49
HUTCHINSON	*	0.00	0.00	0.00	0.00	709.51	227,646.25	1,013.00	125,725.00	172.50	1,895.01

STATE AND UNIT		FISCAL YEAR MBCF ACQUISITION				CUMULATIVE TOTALS AT END OF FISCAL YEAR					
		PURCHASED		EASEMENT OR LEASE		MBCF				ALL OTHER	TOTAL
						PURCHASED		EASEMENT OR LEASE		ACRES	ACRES
		ACRES	COST	ACRES	COST	ACRES	COST	ACRES	COST		
SOUTH DAKOTA											
HYDE	*	0.00	0.00	2,362.53	280,710.00	0.00	0.00	24,616.37	1,979,255.00	3,213.26	27,829.63
JERAULD	*	0.00	0.00	89.00	13,510.00	1,430.40	217,041.00	20,795.98	1,662,490.00	725.40	22,911.73
JONES FSA	** *	0.00	0.00	0.00	0.00	0.00	0.00	0.00	0.00	252.00	252.00
KINGSBURY	*	0.00	0.00	1,068.11	274,445.00	5,256.36	1,258,255.50	22,722.59	2,137,303.00	2,751.57	30,730.52
LAKE	*	0.00	0.00	1,008.58	547,370.00	5,584.50	1,199,017.79	5,511.85	1,110,820.00	852.74	11,949.09
LINCOLN		0.00	0.00	0.00	0.00	177.22	39,925.00	300.50	112,645.00	0.00	477.72
MARSHALL	*	0.00	0.00	1,062.55	128,670.00	10,364.79	1,925,929.00	55,499.52	3,659,508.00	654.88	66,519.19
MCCOOK	*	0.00	0.00	576.00	200,070.00	3,562.96	600,845.60	6,294.00	864,200.00	855.37	10,492.33
MCPHERSON	*	0.00	0.00	1,770.86	118,285.00	19,242.61	3,578,586.80	126,887.56	6,089,480.00	9,280.24	155,410.21
MINER	*	0.00	0.00	1,382.12	454,035.00	1,537.04	151,040.00	18,274.12	2,615,390.00	1,299.80	21,110.96
MINNEHAHA	*	0.00	0.00	0.00	0.00	4,488.84	1,096,786.00	1,640.96	351,295.00	10.00	6,139.80
MOODY	*	0.00	0.00	2.00	990.00	2,903.78	907,478.89	775.00	177,655.00	705.89	4,384.67
POTTER	*	0.00	0.00	10.00	3,100.00	652.63	71,179.00	22,786.23	1,268,545.00	415.10	23,853.96
ROBERTS	*	0.00	0.00	334.00	32,750.00	5,032.73	625,710.80	48,506.78	2,739,803.00	2,255.70	55,795.21
SANBORN	*	0.00	0.00	429.62	100,910.00	95.00	5,250.00	35,418.85	2,872,195.00	535.40	36,047.25
SPINK	*	0.00	0.00	520.00	31,300.00	2,226.43	308,680.00	24,961.65	2,631,961.00	992.90	28,180.98
STANLEY FSA	** *	0.00	0.00	0.00	0.00	0.00	0.00	0.00	0.00	1,404.80	1,404.80
SULLY	*	0.00	0.00	2,784.81	292,060.00	266.48	9,995.00	3,474.81	384,840.00	334.70	4,075.99
TRIPP FSA	** *	0.00	0.00	0.00	0.00	0.00	0.00	0.00	0.00	5.90	5.90
TURNER	*	0.00	0.00	0.00	0.00	850.09	430,044.90	355.00	106,090.00	126.90	1,329.99
UNION		0.00	0.00	0.00	0.00	96.02	22,351.00	0.00	0.00	0.00	96.02
WALWORTH	*	0.00	0.00	38.00	3,320.00	1,524.54	191,800.00	16,793.12	1,168,590.00	553.30	18,870.96
YANKTON		0.00	0.00	0.00	0.00	294.63	128,562.00	125.00	5,375.00	223.50	641.13
TOTAL	44	941.63	622,466.50	36,087.24	5,994,790.00	146,637.84	27,618,567.49	1,027,251.87	73,657,459.00	49,819.06	1,223,708.77
WISCONSIN											
ADAMS		0.00	0.00	0.00	0.00	344.00	172,500.00	0.00	0.00	0.00	344.00
COLUMBIA		76.92	264,000.00	0.00	0.00	2,922.43	2,336,666.45	0.00	0.00	0.00	2,922.43
DANE		38.90	72,000.00	0.00	0.00	1,536.58	1,964,875.65	0.00	0.00	55.50	1,592.08
DODGE		9.00	44,000.00	0.00	0.00	762.45	647,371.14	.43	1,000.00	92.96	855.84
DUNN		0.00	0.00	0.00	0.00	471.18	902,200.00	0.00	0.00	150.80	621.98
FOND DU LAC		1.50	2,250.00	0.00	0.00	578.18	661,767.00	0.00	0.00	255.77	833.95
JEFFERSON		0.00	0.00	0.00	0.00	249.79	241,259.00	0.00	0.00	0.00	249.79
MANITOWOC		0.00	0.00	0.00	0.00	120.00	86,000.00	0.00	0.00	0.00	120.00
MARQUETTE		0.00	0.00	0.00	0.00	259.97	119,480.00	0.00	0.00	0.00	259.97
OZAUKEE		0.00	0.00	0.00	0.00	556.30	679,413.40	0.00	0.00	0.00	556.30
POLK		0.00	0.00	0.00	0.00	845.09	417,426.00	0.00	0.00	199.98	1,045.07
ROCK		52.72	81,000.00	0.00	0.00	349.32	302,358.71	0.00	0.00	0.00	349.32
SHEBOYGAN		213.87	669,636.94	0.00	0.00	329.38	788,636.94	0.00	0.00	208.60	537.98
ST. CROIX		32.71	182,190.00	0.00	0.00	4,872.49	4,999,404.56	0.00	0.00	220.41	5,092.90
WAUSHARA		0.00	0.00	0.00	0.00	252.30	243,000.00	0.00	6,000.00	0.00	252.30
WINNEBAGO		0.00	0.00	0.00	0.00	1,842.33	1,272,300.00	0.00	0.00	75.94	1,918.27
TOTAL	16	425.42	1,295,086.94	0.00	0.00	16,251.79	15,452,636.87	.43	7,000.00	1,259.96	17,512.18
GRAND TOTAL	205	4,011.61	6,600,844.76	49,052.87	9,031,140.42	664,002.15	176,795,355.66	2,031,774.07	135,971,124.16	245,814.20	2,999,590.42

* - THESE COUNTIES INCLUDE INTEREST TRANSFERRED BY THE FSA
** - DENOTES INTERESTS TRANSFERRED BY THE FSA
FSA - FARM SERVICE AGENCY (FORMERLY FARMERS HOME ADMINISTRATION, DEPARTMENT OF AGRICULTURE)

North American Wetlands Conservation Fund (Summary)
Fiscal Year 2002

The Migratory Bird Conservation Commission approved 101 standard wetland conservation project proposals for funding in Fiscal Year 2002 under the North American Wetlands Conservation Act. A total of $74,531,874 from the North American Wetlands Conservation Fund, together with $261,153,404 in partner funds, are supporting 52 projects in the United States, 31 in Canada, and 18 in Mexico. The following tables provide summary and detailed allocation information.

Fiscal Year 2002
Projects Approved by the Migratory Bird Conservation Commission and Active Under the North American Wetlands Conservation Act

Country	Number of Projects	Act Funds	Partner Funds	Acres Affected
U.S.	52	$44,525,147	$216,950,404	634,590
Canada	31	$27,008,153	$ 37,460,453	7,292,747
Mexico	18	$ 2,998,574	$ 6,742,547	19,035
Total	101	$74,531,874	$261,153,404	7,946,372

Title	State	NAWCA Grant ($)	Non-Fed Match ($)	Non-Fed Non-Match	Other Federal Funds ($)	Total Partners	Total Cost ($)	Total Acres	MBCC Approval
B.K. Leach Memorial Conservation Area Addition	MO	999,998	2,577,845	0	3,085,000	5,662,845	6,662,843	2,909	37,155
Centennial Pothole Venture	MN	1,000,000	2,314,424	0	3,869,291	6,183,715	7,183,715	6,843	37,329
Channeled Scablands Focus Area I	WA	978,641	2,109,488	0	3,161,102	5,270,590	6,249,231	12,370	37,155
Chase Lake Area Wetland Project V	ND	1,000,000	1,000,000	0	297,380	1,297,380	2,297,380	34,295	37,155
Chenier Plain Coastal Wetlands Restoration	LA	999,364	2,145,723	0	10,580	2,156,303	3,155,667	29,237	37,329
Chesapeake Bay Initiative II	DE,MD,PA,VA,WV	533,000	1,532,628	0	0	1,532,628	2,065,628	9,811	37,419
Chickasawhatchee Swamp Habitat Conservation Project	GA	1,000,000	22,315,000	0	0	22,315,000	23,315,000	19,700	37,329
Choctaw Island	AR	300,000	3,165,195	1,348,002	2,867,363	7,380,580	7,680,580	8,300	37,155
Columbia River Estuary Project	OR,WA	997,000	997,119	4,625,000	2,031,434	7,653,553	8,650,553	5,936	37,329
Comprehensive Bird Conservation, Red River Of The North	MN	798,335	2,236,593	4,280	0	2,240,873	3,039,208	3,594	37,329
Connecticut River: Northern Valley Conservation Project	NH,VT	914,000	9,257,000	0	3,500,000	12,757,000	13,671,000	82,829	37,329
East Bay Habitat Protection Project II	RI	1,000,000	3,130,425	0	210,000	3,340,425	4,340,425	507	37,155
East Grand Traverse Bay Wetlands Initiative	MI	1,000,000	3,050,000	0	0	3,050,000	4,050,000	1,104	37,155
Glacial Habitat Restoration Area IV	WI	1,000,000	2,133,280	0	0	2,133,280	3,133,280	3,494	37,329
Grand Bay National Wildlife Refuge	MS	533,000	3,800,000	0	0	3,800,000	4,333,000	2,700	37,419
Green River State Forest	KY	800,000	1,655,150	0	0	1,655,150	2,455,150	1,980	37,329
Heart Of The Chesapeake I	MD	1,000,000	10,653,000	0	0	10,653,000	11,653,000	19,318	37,155
Heart Of The Chesapeake II	MD	991,000	10,650,000	0	0	10,650,000	11,641,000	19,359	37,329
High Plains Wetland Project	SD	880,000	1,873,679	0	250,000	2,123,679	3,013,679	1,932	37,155
Iowa Glaciated Wetlands Initiative	IA	700,000	1,114,717	0	1,016,400	2,131,117	2,831,117	2,789	37,155
Izembek NWR Complex I	AK	1,000,000	2,000,000	0	0	2,000,000	3,000,000	21,565	37,155
Lake St. Clair / Western Lake Erie Watershed Project	MI	1,000,000	2,006,745	317,975	186,952	2,511,672	3,511,672	4,196	37,155
Lewis & Clark Floodplain Heritage Partnership I	MO	970,000	1,888,270	17,120	3,932,625	5,820,895	6,790,895	11,848	37,329
Lower Mississippi Valley Ecosystem III	AR,LA,MS	999,667	3,274,666	0	300,790	3,592,576	4,592,243	44,973	37,329
Lower Obion River I	TN	1,000,000	2,853,994	0	1,833,000	4,686,994	5,686,994	5,807	37,329
McPherson Valley Wetlands IV	KS	557,135	1,398,172	0	30,000	1,428,172	1,985,307	1,537	37,155
Michigan Upper Peninsula Coastal Wetland II	MI	833,817	1,947,685	0	1,363,632	3,258,692	4,092,509	3,309	37,155
Mid - Mississippi Alluvial Valley Bird Conservation Area I	TN	1,000,000	3,075,900	0	2,243,751	5,319,651	6,319,651	14,033	37,155
Middle Rio Grande Wetlands Project	NM	1,000,000	2,075,660	0	125,427	2,201,087	3,201,087	2,637	37,155
Middle Willamette Valley Floodplain Protection Project	OR	901,400	1,660,000	244,275	349,300	2,253,575	3,154,975	1,990	37,155
Missouri Coteau Habitat Conservation Project III	ND	800,000	839,247	0	0	839,247	1,639,247	43,329	37,329
Mobile - Tensaw Delta III	AL	1,000,000	4,068,200	1,845,000	0	5,913,200	6,913,200	12,682	37,329
Montana Hi-Line Prairie Wetland Project	MT	1,000,000	1,947,685	0	799,375	2,747,060	3,747,060	59,770	37,155
N. Delaware Wetlands Rehab Program - Old Wilmington Marsh	DE	891,000	1,877,500	0	0	1,877,500	2,768,500	202	37,155
North Dakota Great Plains III	ND	200,000	202,184	0	166,587	368,771	568,771	348	37,329
Northwest Ohio Wetlands Initiative	OH	1,000,000	4,241,348	0	1,135,000	5,376,348	6,376,348	3,052	37,329
Port Bolivar Wetlands Protection	TX	450,000	475,500	5,000	36,000	516,500	966,500	1,365	37,329
Paso Creek Flood Plain Wetland Habitat Project	CA	1,000,000	1,665,557	0	4,901,183	6,566,740	7,566,740	9,306	37,329
Rainwater Basin (East) Partnership Project	NE	724,610	984,610	0	1,678,327	2,662,937	3,387,547	5,683	37,155
Rocky Mountain Front Protection Project I	MT	1,000,000	2,906,206	13,000	1,726,411	4,645,617	5,645,617	24,897	37,329
Skagit / Samish Priority Wetlands Habitat Prot. & Rest. II	WA	922,068	1,900,844	0	126,000	2,026,844	2,948,912	1,945	37,329
South Park Valley Premier Wetlands & Mountain Plover Habitat	CO	1,000,000	1,566,000	1,200,000	0	2,766,000	3,766,000	10,217	37,329
South Shore Grays Harbor Project	WA	955,000	1,948,800	0	100,000	2,048,800	3,003,800	1,001	37,155

UNITED STATES WETLANDS CONSERVATION STANDARD GRANT PROPOSALS
APPROVED BY THE MIGRATORY BIRD CONSERVATION COMMISSION
FOR FISCAL YEAR 2002
TABLE THREE

Project	State								
Southeast Virginia Watersheds Project II	VA	502,974	1,059,165	0	1,352,363	2,411,528	2,914,502	1,247	37,155
Southeast Wisconsin Coastal Habitat Initiative III	WI	995,638	2,112,949	0	0	2,112,949	3,108,587	2,642	37,155
Steptoe Valley Wetlands	NV	500,000	1,014,672	16,700	5,000	1,036,372	1,536,372	6,426	37,155
The Port Susan Bay All Bird Initiative	WA	955,000	955,000	40,000	0	995,000	1,950,000	4,122	37,155
Threatened Habitats Project	SD	905,000	990,000	0	5,400,000	6,390,000	7,295,000	57,696	37,155
West Eugene - Long Tom Target Area	OR	1,000,000	2,622,159	91,760	8,669,900	11,383,819	12,383,819	981	37,329
Wetlands Restoration Within The West Gulf Coastal Plain	TX	467,500	953,840	0	426,800	1,380,640	1,848,140	3,520	37,155
Whitehurst Marsh Acquisition II	VA	1,000,000	4,368,079	0	0	4,368,079	5,368,079	2,610	37,329
Wood River Roost Wetland	NE	560,000	901,711	499,070	55,240	1,456,021	2,016,021	648	37,329
Fiscal Year 2002 Totals Number of Projects 52		44,525,147	149,440,989	10,267,182	57,242,233	216,950,404	261,475,551	634,590	
U.S. SMALL GRANTS									
Fiscal Year 2002 Totals Number of Projects 42		1,931,799	8,955,538	1,958,634	2,222,519	13,136,691	15,068,490	11,708	

CANADIAN WETLANDS CONSERVATION PROPOSALS
APPROVED BY THE MIGRATORY BIRD CONSERVATION COMMISSION
FOR FISCAL YEAR 2002
TABLE FOUR

Title	Province	NAWCA Grant ($)	U.S. Match ($)	Canadian Partners ($)	Total Partners ($)	Total Cost ($)	Total Acres	MBCC Approval
Alberta - Critical Wetland & Upland Habitat	AB	632,306	632,306	421,537	1,053,843	1,686,149	9,500	37,419
Alberta Habitat Program	AB,BC	2,949,750	2,949,750	464,400	3,414,150	6,363,900	33,800	37,419
Alberta Habitat Program	AB,BC	3,191,250	3,191,250	579,600	3,770,850	6,962,100	28,987	37,155
Bay Of Fundy Habitat Securement Project	NB,NS	199,800	199,800	132,975	332,775	532,575	600	37,419
Coastal & Intermountain British Columbia	BC	690,916	690,916	675,000	1,365,916	2,056,832	950	37,419
Cons Of Wetlands & Assoc Upland Habitats Coastal & Intermoun	BC	621,690	621,690	207,000	828,690	1,450,380	515	37,155
Critical British Columbia Coastal & Intermountain Wetland Habitats	BC	912,241	912,241	675,000	1,587,241	2,499,482	3,375	37,419
Manitoba - Critical Upland & Wetland Habitat	MB	658,125	658,125	438,750	1,096,875	1,755,000	8,960	37,419
Manitoba Prairie Parkland Program	MB	1,251,450	1,251,450	36,450	1,287,900	2,539,350	9,337	37,419
Manitoba Prairie Parkland Program	MB	1,595,280	1,595,280	41,400	1,636,680	3,231,960	9,111	37,155
New Brunswick Wetlands	NB	175,950	175,950	124,200	300,150	476,100	1,496	37,419
New Brunswick Wetlands Conservation	NB	172,125	172,125	128,925	301,050	473,175	1,127	37,419
Newfoundland & Labrador Coastal & Inland Freshwater Wetlands	NF	51,300	51,300	45,225	96,525	147,825	610	37,419
Newfoundland & Labrador Coastal & Inland Freshwater Wetlands	NF	56,580	56,580	37,950	94,530	151,110	790	37,155
Nova Scotia Coastal & Inland Wetlands	NS	120,825	120,825	100,575	221,400	342,225	722	37,419
Nova Scotia Coastal & Inland Wetlands	NS	127,650	127,650	84,870	212,520	340,170	1,221	37,155
Ontario Regional Project	ON	742,440	742,440	494,730	1,237,170	1,979,610	1,215	37,419
Ontario Regional Project	ON	899,775	899,775	614,250	1,514,025	2,413,800	1,490	37,419
Ontario Wetland Habitat Conservation Project	ON	337,500	337,500	224,842	562,342	899,842	1,000	37,419
Ontario Wetland Habitat Fund Program	ON	138,000	138,000	333,891	471,891	609,891	4,000	37,155
Potholes Plus Project	MB	425,925	425,925	192,375	618,300	1,044,225	6,350	37,419
Prince Edward Island Wetlands In The Agricultural Landscape	PE	88,320	88,320	155,250	243,570	331,890	1,371	37,155
Prince Edward Island Wetlands In The Agricultural Landscape	PE	105,975	105,975	98,550	204,525	310,500	1,028	37,419
Quebec / St. Lawrence & Adjoining Landscapes	QC	440,220	440,220	370,530	810,750	1,250,970	7,000	37,155
Quebec / St. Lawrence & Adjoining Landscapes	QC	449,550	449,550	309,825	759,375	1,208,925	2,500	37,419
Saskatchewan Critical Wetland & Upland Habitat	SK	632,800	632,800	421,900	1,054,700	1,687,500	12,800	37,419
Saskatchewan Habitat Program	SK	2,949,750	2,949,750	216,000	3,165,750	6,115,500	38,650	37,419
Saskatchewan Habitat Program	SK	3,121,560	3,121,560	224,250	3,345,810	6,467,370	36,142	37,155
Saskatchewan Prairie Shores Project	SK	69,000	69,000	138,000	207,000	276,000	17,800	37,155
South Okanagan Key Program Areas	BC	200,100	200,100	138,000	338,100	538,200	300	37,155
Western Boreal Forest Program	AB,BC,MB,NT,NU,SK,YT	3,000,000	3,000,000	2,326,050	5,326,050	8,326,050	7,050,000	37,419
Fiscal Year 2002 Totals Number of Projects 31		27,008,153	27,008,153	10,452,300	37,460,453	64,468,606	7,292,747	

MEXICAN WETLANDS CONSERVATION PROPOSALS
APPROVED BY THE MIGRATORY BIRD CONSERVATION COMMISSION
FOR FISCAL YEAR 2002
TABLE FIVE

Title	State	NAWCA Grant ($)	Non-Fed Match ($)	Non-Fed Non-Match	Other Federal Funds ($)	Total Partners($)	Total Cost ($)	Total Acres	MBCC Approval
A Community Partnership - Rio Hardy - Colorado River Delta	BCN	63,800	63,850	0	0	63,850	127,650	20	37,419
Conservation & Mgmt Of The Wetlands Of Alvarado	VER	339,180	430,960	0	0	430,960	770,140	0	37,419
Development Of A Model For Citizen Participation, Mgt / Rest	VER	119,100	187,367	0	0	187,367	306,467	0	37,155
Durangueno Wetlands	DGO	226,100	474,235	4,200	0	478,435	704,535	1,272	37,419
Ensenada De Pabellones	SIN	136,522	269,350	0	0	269,350	405,872	0	37,329
Envir. Status Eval. Playas De Catazaja II	CHIS,TAB	89,868	105,978	0	0	105,978	195,846	0	37,329
Estab. Of Res. Mgt. Monitoring, Visitor Ctr. Acq Of Pez Maya	Q.ROO	400,000	2,746,000	0	0	2,746,000	3,146,000	64	37,155
Estab. Of An Environmental Mgt. Unit, Alvarado Wetland	VER	192,668	712,348	0	0	712,348	905,016	0	37,419
Planning, Municipal Ecol Policies & Resource Devel, Tuxpan	VER	49,650	51,091	0	0	51,091	100,741	0	37,155
Purchase Of Land Rights, Bird & Wildlife Habitat, N. Yucatan	YUC	249,300	258,006	0	0	258,006	507,306	4,940	37,155
Rancho El Hermalbo	TAMPS	56,707	74,026	0	0	74,026	130,733	140	37,329
Regionalization Of The PIE, Coastal Wetlands In Nw Mexico	BCN,BCS,NAY,SIN	149,132	236,800	0	0	236,800	385,932	0	37,155
Restauracion De Cobertura Vegetal, El Palmar, II	YUC	153,543	155,000	0	0	155,000	308,543	12,500	37,155
Restoration Of Cienega De San Bernardino Watershed	SON	369,574	500,000	0	0	500,000	869,574	0	37,329
San Crisanto, A Sustainable Development Project	YUC	68,208	68,411	0	0	68,411	136,619	99	37,329
The 2002 Veracruz Model	CHIS	65,000	112,675	0	2,000	114,675	179,675	0	37,329
Well Cons Corridor, Pacific Coastal Plain Of Chiapas - Oaxaca	CHIS,OAX	192,392	199,537	0	0	199,537	391,929	0	37,155
Wetlands Of Importance For The Arctic Goose In Mexico II	CHIH,COAH,DGO,NL,TAMPS,ZAC	77,830	87,713	0	3,000	90,713	168,543	0	37,329
Fiscal Year 2002 Totals Number of Projects 18		2,998,574	6,733,347	4,200	5,000	6,742,547	9,741,121	19,035	

www.ingramcontent.com/pod-product-compliance
Lightning Source LLC
Chambersburg PA
CBHW070844310526
45793CB00011B/531